Brainstorming and Beyond

Brainstorming and Beyond

A User-Centered Design Method

Chauncey Wilson

AMSTERDAM • BOSTON • HEIDELBERG • LONDON
NEW YORK • OXFORD • PARIS • SAN DIEGO
SAN FRANCISCO • SINGAPORE • SYDNEY • TOKYO
Morgan Kaufmann is an imprint of Elsevier

Morgan Kaufmann is an imprint of Elsevier
The Boulevard, Langford Lane, Kidlington, Oxford, OX5 1GB, UK
225 Wyman Street, Waltham, MA 02451, USA

First published 2013

British Library Cataloguing-in-Publication Data
A catalogue record for this book is available from the British Library

Library of Congress Cataloging-in-Publication Data
A catalog record for this book is available from the Library of Congress

ISBN: 978-0-12-407157-5

For information on all Morgan Kaufmann publications
visit our website at store.elsevier.com

This book has been manufactured using Print On Demand technology. Each copy is produced
to order and is limited to black ink. The online version of this book will show color figures
where appropriate.

Working together to grow
libraries in developing countries

www.elsevier.com | www.bookaid.org | www.sabre.org

ELSEVIER   BOOK AID
International   Sabre Foundation

CONTENTS

INTRODUCTION

If I have a thousand ideas and only one turns out to be good, I am satisfied.
Alfred Nobel

Most projects spend considerable resources generating and organizing ideas throughout the product cycle. The three chapters in this book describe effective and efficient methods for generating ideas through speaking, writing, and drawing.

Chapter 1 in this book focuses on group brainstorming, perhaps the most well-known method for ideation. Brainstorming is often portrayed as simple with only a few rules, but as you read through the first chapter, you will discover that brainstorming is a complex social process requiring knowledge of social psychology, motivation, and corporate culture. There are many variations on brainstorming that can be useful in different contexts, like the nominal group technique, which is useful when you want to minimize status differences, and "free listing," which can be used to generate ideas with very large groups (as well as with a single individual) in minutes. This chapter provides many tips on how you can increase the number of ideas that emerge from brainstorming sessions.

Chapter 2 describes a method called "brainwriting." Brainwriting is a variation on brainstorming, in which each person in a group writes ideas on paper and then passes the paper to another who reads the first set of ideas and adds new ones. Brainwriting requires little training and could be considered a "discount" ideation method. Because there is no group where participants shout out ideas, strong facilitation skills are not required for the leader of a brainwriting session. The output of ideas from brainwriting can often exceed the output of group brainstorming in a shorter period of time, so the return on investment (in this case, the number of ideas per unit time) is relatively high compared to traditional group brainstorming. Brainwriting is appropriate in cultures where there is some hostility (covert or overt) or where participants may be reluctant to express ideas that go against the ideas of more senior colleagues. It is also useful when you have limited time with a group.

Chapter 3 covers braindrawing, a method of visual brainstorming that you can use to generate ideas for icons, graphics for product branding, user interface layouts, or web page designs. In braindrawing, you present a group with a visual problem like "generate ideas for an icon to represent the function 'insert link', and then ask each person to sketch ideas and pass them on to someone else who can add a new idea or embellish previous ideas." Good ideas are extracted from braindrawings and applied in the product.

The methods described in this book provide ways to generate, present, and evaluate ideas and begin building a strong foundation for product success.

Brainstorming

1.7 WHAT DO YOU NEED FOR BRAINSTORMING?
1.7.1 Personnel, Participants, and Training
1.7.2 Hardware and Software
1.7.3 Documents and Materials
RECOMMENDED READINGS
REFERENCES

Alternate names: Brainstorming, creative thinking, group brainstorming, group ideation, interactive brainstorming.

Related methods: Affinity diagramming, braindrawing, brainwriting, buzz group, Delphi technique, individual brainstorming, KJ method, metaphor brainstorming, nominal group technique, remote brainstorming, unstructured brainstorming, and visual brainstorming.

1.1 OVERVIEW OF BRAINSTORMING

Brainstorming is an individual or group method for generating ideas, increasing creative efficacy, or finding solutions to problems. This chapter focuses on group brainstorming where participants generate ideas on a particular topic or problem in a nonjudgmental environment following a set of ground rules about appropriate behaviors. Table 1.1 is a method scorecard that highlights the relative investment needed to conduct a group brainstorming session and when brainstorming is most useful.

The basic procedure for group brainstorming involves:

1. Selecting a group of three to ten participants with different backgrounds.
2. Posing a clear problem, question, or topic to the group.

Table 1.1 Method Scorecard for Brainstorming

Overall effort required	Time for planning and conducting	Skill and experience	Supplies and equipment	Time for data analysis

Most useful during these project phases:				
✓ Problem definition	✓ Requirements	✓ Conceptual design	Detailed design	Implementation

3. Asking the group to generate solutions or ideas with no criticism or attempts to limit the type and number of ideas. This is the "divergent" phase in which you want as many ideas as possible without any censorship.
4. Discussing, critiquing, and possibly prioritizing the brainstorming results for later action. This last step is often called the "convergent" phase where there is a winnowing of all the ideas into the ones that are judged as most applicable to a problem.

Variations on group brainstorming can be used to gather ideas from large groups, geographically-dispersed people, or participants who are inhibited by their shyness, the social environment, or cultural norms. These variations are described later in this chapter.

Alex Osborn, an advertising executive, is generally credited with developing modern organizational brainstorming procedures in the 1940s and 1950s (Osborn, 1963). Osborn described brainstorming (originally he called it "thinking up") in his classic book, *Applied Imagination: Principles and Procedures of Creative Problem-Solving.*

"Brainstorms" as Mental Disease and Fortunate Thoughts

In the early part of the twentieth century, "brainstorm" referred to violent bouts of temper or bouts of lethargy and depression. Toward the middle of the twentieth century, the usage of "brainstorm" changed to mean "sudden and fortunate thoughts" (Oxford English Dictionary, 2012). Alex Osborn, the "father of brainstorming" used the term "brainstorm session" in the mid-1950s to describe his method of generating solutions to problems (Osborn, 1963).

There are three fundamental principles for group brainstorming:

1. **Aim for sheer quantity.** Quantity, not quality, is the goal of brainstorming. The primary criterion for the success of brainstorming is the sheer number of ideas that are generated.

   Anything that limits the number of ideas is contrary to the intent of brainstorming. For example, brainstorming participants should not be taking their own notes because that keeps them (and those around them) from generating ideas. Participants should not be monitoring e-mail (so easy now with wireless connections, smartphones, and tablets!) or checking out Facebook during brainstorming. After the brainstorming session, you can criticize, rate, rank, or vote on what makes a good idea, but during brainstorming the focus should be on getting as many ideas as possible.

2. **Defer judgment about the quality of ideas.** Do not criticize the ideas of others either implicitly (e.g., through facial expressions or other nonverbal behaviors) or explicitly (saying "Wow! That is a crazy idea!").

3. **Encourage new and wild ideas.** New ideas can be generated by synthesizing ideas, stretching ideas (bigger, faster, smaller), applying metaphors, or improving on existing ideas. Wild ideas that may not be directly applicable to a brainstorming topic can serve as triggers for ideas that are potentially useful. Ideas from science fiction stories or movies, for example, might seem odd, but many existing products are filled with concepts like teleportation, invisibility, and the ability to travel back in time (Freeman & Gelernter, 1996).

The apparent simplicity of these three principles leads many people to assume that successful brainstorming is easy and can be done by anyone. However, this assumption is not always warranted. Good brainstorming is rare, and in many cases what people consider "good brainstorming" is often seriously deficient. More on that later.

●●●─────────────────────────────────────

Tip

During a brainstorming session, should you praise people for ideas? The answer would generally be "No!".

While the rule to avoid criticism during brainstorming is well known, another more subtle rule is to avoid praise. Praising an idea is attaching a judgment to that idea which means that the lack of praise for other ideas could be construed as tacit criticism. So, avoid both praise and criticism during brainstorming.

───────────────────────────────────────

Osborn's "structured brainstorming" approach, with clear ground rules and procedures, contrasts with "unstructured brainstorming," where a group gets together to generate ideas without a facilitator or clear ground rules (Osborn, 1963). Ideas that emerge from unstructured brainstorming are often criticized as they are generated, and loud or dominant individuals can exert inordinate influence on the quiet participants, thus limiting the number and type of ideas that participants are willing to express. This chapter will focus on structured brainstorming where there is generally a facilitator and a set of explicit rules for participants.

Don't Believe All That You Read on the Web: Group Brainstorming Isn't Simple!

While group brainstorming seems simple, there are many social issues like status differences, shyness, informal relationships, ego, and cultural factors that can affect the quantity of ideas. Camacho and Paulus (1995, p. 1078) found, for example, that social anxiety had a significant effect on brainstorming productivity and suggested that "... interactive [group] brainstorming may be best suited for people who are low in social anxiety".

A trained facilitator can mitigate some of these problems, but even a good facilitator won't have total insight into all the social forces and group dynamics that can influence productivity. Sandberg (2006), writing in *The Wall Street Journal*, summarizes some key requirements for successful group brainstorming:

"In fact, great brainstorming sessions are possible, but they require the planning of a state dinner, plenty of rules, and the suspension of ego, ingratiation and political railroading."

1.2 WHEN SHOULD YOU USE BRAINSTORMING?

Use brainstorming to:

- generate ideas or requirements;
- find solutions to specific problems;
- support conceptual design by generating metaphors, ideas for user interface (UI) architectures, and new ways to do old things;
- explore new design spaces;
- generate social cohesion within product teams.

Brainstorming is often used in the early to middle stages of product development; however, this method is applicable any time that new ideas or solutions to problems are required. If you have an unexpected and difficult problem just before you release a product, brainstorming would be an appropriate method for generating potential solutions.

1.2.1 Strengths
- Brainstorming has name recognition. Most people have some sense of what a group brainstorming session is like and you don't have to convince teams to use the method (which you might if you decide to try a lesser known approach like brainwriting).

- Provides ideas that may not surface any other way.
- Provides many ideas quickly.
- Requires few material resources. Paper, pens, sticky notes, and tape are about all you need unless you are doing remote brainstorming.
- Is a useful way to get over design blocks that are holding up a project.
- Is a democratic way of generating ideas (assuming that particular people don't dominate and you have a good facilitator).
- Provides social interaction—people like to work together in groups to solve problems.

1.2.2 Weaknesses

- Is sometimes less effective than having the same number of participants generating ideas individually. The quantity of ideas can suffer when one person in the brainstorming group blocks the production of ideas by other participants by telling "war stories" or whispering to a colleague. Brainwriting, covered in Chapter 2, can yield a trove of ideas using a silent method where participants write ideas on slips and hand them in or pass them to someone else who adds additional new ideas or modifies previous ones.
- There is often no good way to match ideas that come up in brainstorming with an insight that occurs outside the brainstorming room that might just be the missing ingredient to a brilliant concept. Johnson (2010), in his book, *Where Good Ideas Come From*, suggests that groups build information networks that allow ideas from different times and places to mix and provide brilliant insights.
- Requires an experienced facilitator who is sensitive to group dynamics and social pressures and not afraid to note violations of the ground rules.
- The focus on the quantity of ideas can be derailed easily by criticism or poor facilitation.
- Can be chaotic and intimidating to the quiet or shy person.
- Can reduce individual recognition for good ideas (although you can compensate for this by being known as a "good brainstormer" and creative contributor).
- May be difficult in some corporations, countries, or cultures where "wild ideas" could be viewed as inappropriate because those ideas are contrary to corporate initiatives or cultural norms.

- Status or experience differences among participants can reduce brainstorming effectiveness. Mixing senior and junior colleagues may cause junior people to defer to their more senior colleagues.
- Sorting through hundreds of ideas and choosing the best ones can be difficult.

1.3 PROCEDURES AND PRACTICAL ADVICE ON BRAINSTORMING

1.3.1 Planning the Brainstorming Session

1. **Decide if group brainstorming is going to be the best method for generating ideas or solutions for your particular question.** Other ways to generate ideas, like spirited debate, brainwriting, braindrawing, free listing, scanning ideas from previous activities, or idea networks where colleagues share and rate ideas of others, might be more appropriate for some contexts. For example, if you have some quiet people who might feel intimidated because their managers want to be part of the brainstorming session, you might try a less public method like brainwriting (Chapter 2).

Tip

Brainstorming homework can focus the creative energies of your participants, but asking people to do homework creates some obligations for the participants AND facilitator.

1. Assign homework that is reasonable given the roles and schedules of your participants.
2. Make sure that you give people enough time to complete the homework.
3. Make the homework fun!
4. Give your participants clear instructions about what they should do with the results of the homework—for example, jot down answers to a brainstorming question based on the homework. You might ask people to bring examples to the session for inspiration.
5. Make it clear that the participants are expected to come to the meeting, homework-in-hand.

2. **Develop the question or topic that will be the focus of the brainstorming session.** The topic should be neither overly broad ("What can

we do to make consumer products better?") nor so narrow ("What color should we use for the background of the horizontal navigation bar in our web site?") that creativity is stifled (Wellner, 2003). The topic could be focused on a specific customer problem or need like "What can we do to reduce the time it takes to become proficient with our product?"

3. **Decide if there is some "homework" for the brainstorming session that will prime the participants and encourage more ideas.** You might expose your colleagues to stimuli related to your brainstorming topic. Kelley (2001, p. 60), for example, describes a warm-up "experiment" for a brainstorming session at IDEO on toy design that involved different types of homework. One group of designers did no preparation for the session; a second group read books related to the design of toys and listened to a lecture; the third group took a field trip to a toy store. Each group conducted a brainstorming exercise. According to Kelley, the group that actually went to the toy store generated more and better ideas than the other two groups. This was not a definitive study, but asking a group to step outside their current experience provides an opening for more ideas. Nowadays, research is relatively easy since you can use Google to collect information, examine images, and read scholarly articles on nearly everything.

4. **Choose a facilitator who has experience conducting brainstorming sessions or similar activities like focus groups or design reviews.** If you have a contentious group with some overpowering participants, consider a facilitator with formal training. Brainstorming sessions are enhanced by experienced facilitators who can focus on eliciting as many ideas as possible and reminding participants of the ground rules.

5. **Draft an agenda for the brainstorming session that describes how much time is allocated to introductions, discussion of the topic and procedure, warm-up exercises, the brainstorming itself, and any post-brainstorming activities.** A common question about brainstorming is "how long should the actual brainstorming session last?" The answers in the literature range from 15 minutes to several hours per topic with frequent short breaks when there are sessions longer than 30 minutes. Short breaks may help overcome mental blocks or fixations on particular approaches or solutions. Some brainstorming researchers advocate giving participants cards to write ideas on during the breaks from active brainstorming.

6. **Decide on the size and composition of the group.** A group of three to ten participants is recommended, although if you have a large group, you might consider a variation called the "buzz group" or "buzz session" (described later in this chapter) where you split a large group into smaller groups of three to six participants. These buzz groups each conduct their own brainstorming sessions, report the results to everyone (Brahm & Kleiner, 1996), and then all the ideas from different sessions are combined into a single list. If there is a mix of managers and employees, the managers can brainstorm in their own group so they don't intimidate those who work for them.

It is advantageous to have a somewhat diverse group to explore ideas from different perspectives, but be careful about the mix of participants. Try to invite participants who are about the same rank in the organization to avoid status anxiety. If you invite outsiders—people who are not known to the main group—introduce them with a bit of background and do some warm-up exercises before you get started with the official brainstorming topic.

Diversity Can Be Good or Bad

Diversity is important, but group comfort and cohesion are also important for successful brainstorming (Milliken & Martins, 1996). Brainstorming guidelines often call for diverse participants on the assumption that greater diversity will yield more diverse ideas. This is true to a point, but diversity can also create problems for brainstorming.

The relationship between diversity and creativity is complex; sometimes diversity in groups can lead to discomfort (Milliken, Bartel, & Kurtzberg, 2003). For example, having several senior managers and strangers from other parts of a company join you for a brainstorming session might increase diversity, but also make the junior participants feel awkward or anxious about voicing "bad" or "wild" or "politically incorrect" ideas in front of other managers or strangers.

Some 10–15 minutes warm-up exercises you might consider to reduce anxiety are:

a. A practice brainstorming session on a topic that is not at all associated with the job or the topic of the session. You might invite people to brainstorm about "new kitchen gadgets" or "new applications for smartphones." The practice topic should be fun, something that everyone can relate to, and stimulating enough for a brisk 10 minutes or so of idea generation.

b. An exercise where you hold up an item like a brick or paper clip, or show a photo of a common object and ask people to brainstorm as many ways to use the object as possible. A brick, for example, could be used as a paperweight, prototype, weapon, chicken-flattener, door stop, exercise device, or hammer.

c. A word association exercise where you give people a word like "apple" or "strong" and ask the group to list as many associations with the word as possible e.g., with "apple" you might get: gravity, Fuji, computer company, pie, doctor, health, crisp, record, Beatles, California, juice, fritter, and jack.

●●●————————————————————————————————

Tip

To make it easier for a person in a brainstorming session, you might post your ground rules and on the wall and after reviewing them together, clearly state: "I (the facilitator) will point out any violation of the ground rules and gently remind the group. If any of you feel that someone is not abiding by the rules, you can point that out at any time." This author was conducting a brainstorming session once and made a subtle ground rule transgression and a colleague very gently reminded me of my rule violation. Even good facilitators need an occasional reminder about the ground rules.

7. **Choose a location that is comfortable and has flipcharts and space on the walls for posting ideas.** Try to get a room other than the room where you meet everyday to talk about boring topics like the daily bug reports or changes to the project plan (Berkun, 2004). If this is a crucial session, you might want to get your participants out of their building and away from possible interruptions (any interruptions will reduce the quantity of ideas).

   In larger cities, there are often companies that will rent out rooms for half days. Convince your participants not to bring their laptops and to put their mobile phones in silent mode. You do not want participants answering calls, checking e-mails, whispering to each other, or doing other work during brainstorming. Each interruption takes time away from idea generation and blocks the production of new ideas for both the individual and group.

8. **Develop a short introduction (several minutes is often enough) that describes brainstorming and your goals for the session.** A checklist of items for the introduction would include:
   - Introducing yourself and your role as facilitator.
   - Describing the goal of the session.
   - Laying out the timeline for the session.
   - Describing the process.
   - Describing the ground rules and how they will be enforced (this is very important).
   - Describing what you will do with the data.
   - Conducting a brief warm-up.

9. **Develop an explicit set of rules for the brainstorming session and go over them during your introduction.** Paulus and Brown (2003, p. 130) and other experts have proposed rules for productive brainstorming sessions. Here is a set of ground rules based on both research and personal experience that this author has used with success.

Ground Rules for Brainstorming
Quantity, not quality, is the goal of the session
No criticism and no praise
Wild and different ideas are welcome
Don't worry about duplicates
You can modify the ideas of others
No long stories (that takes time away from ideas)
You can ask for brief clarification if you don't understand an idea, abbreviation, or term.
Ground rules will be posted and enforced
Anyone can note a violation of ground rules
Cell phones on vibrate and no computers or tablets except for the notetaker
Only one person speaks at a time
If you have an idea while someone else is speaking, write the idea down on a sticky note

10. **Ensure that all the ideas generated during brainstorming are visible to everyone.** The facilitator or a designated notetaker should be writing the ideas down on large sheets of paper or large sticky notes so everyone can see all the ideas. Write the ideas large enough and legibly enough for the person furthest away in the room to read them easily. Avoid typing ideas into a computer and displaying them to the participants unless you are doing sessions

with colleagues at different sites. Even with high-resolution displays, only a few dozen ideas will generally be visible which reduces the likelihood of early ideas triggering later ideas.

11. **Develop some techniques for encouraging new ideas and expanding existing ones.** Osborn (1963) provided a checklist of techniques for changing and expanding ideas during a brainstorming session. This venerable, but still relevant, checklist includes the following techniques:

   - **Adapt.** Is there something like this idea that might be worth emulating? Could you adapt a concept from physics or psychology or cooking to expand on an idea?

   - **Modify.** Can you change something about the idea? What would happen if you changed color, materials, shape, motion, visual style, orientation, texture, or who the users are?

   - **Magnify.** What happens if you add things to your idea or change some properties? What could you do to make it larger, faster, heavier, taller, wider, or sexier? What if you accentuated various properties like saturation or brightness? What if two or more people could use something that is currently a single person system?

   - **Minify.** Can you subtract things from an idea? Can you make it smaller, shorter, lighter, or more condensed? Can you subtract features? Can you reduce complexity? Can you eliminate features? Can you shrink something in a single dimension?

   - **Put to other uses.** Can you put your idea to some other use? What else could you do with the idea beyond the immediate use? For example, what nonstandard uses could you come up with for a set of features in a graphics program?

   - **Substitute.** Can you interchange components, methods, techniques, ingredients, people, language, perspective, or something else? For example, you might take the perspective of someone who was 80 years old with arthritis, poor vision from macular degeneration, and hearing problems.

   - **Rearrange.** Can you use a different organization, layout, sequence, or arrangement? Can you move things around? Can you invert or reverse the order of controls in a user interface? Berkun (2004) proposes several other "tricks" for stimulating new ideas during brainstorming sessions.

- **Use random theme generators.** Here you might have a list of random words, attributes, colors, shapes, or other stimuli that you use for design brainstorming. You would pull out random sets of words and ask how you would design something with these attributes.
- **Eliminate constraints.** Explicitly remove common barriers like cost, current technology, schedule, safety features, and expertise, and see what ideas emerge when people are not operating with assumptions about everyday constraints. What could you do if you removed some of the things that the development team said "the development kit doesn't support"?
- **Add constraints.** Here you might impose constraints and generate ideas that fall within those constraints. For example, you might add a constraint that the product must work "under water," "in bright desert sun," or "in a hurricane." If you add the constraint that the product (and user) will sometimes be subject to intense vibration, you might come up with ideas for using a product in vehicles or while riding a bicycle.
- **"Rotate."** Berkun (2004) suggests adding a bit of physicality to brainstorming by asking people to get up and move one chair to the right or left. The rationale for rotating seating position is that a surprise physical action might loosen the participants up and inject a bit of levity and energy into the session. Rotating is potentially risky if your colleagues lack a sense of play in the workplace. Before trying actions that are clearly unusual like rotating seats, consider your audience carefully.

If you will be called on to facilitate brainstorming sessions or focus groups, keep a list of these methods with brief instructions on how to apply them if a brainstorming session starts to lose energy. These creativity stimulation techniques take practice, so try some of them out on a small and friendly group first. You can find other techniques for idea generation in books on creativity and design.

Where to Find Some Creativity Techniques and Tips for Facilitators

There are many books out with techniques for stimulating the creativity of your colleagues including:

Epstein, R. (1996). *Creativity games for trainers: A handbook of group activities for jump-starting workplace creativity*. New York, NY: McGraw-Hill.

The Forensic Technician. *100 online brainstorming tools to help you think outside the box.* <http://www.forensicsciencetechnician.org/100-online-brainstorming-tools-to-help-you-think-outside-the-box/> Accessed 28.10.12.

Gray, Brown and Macanufo (2010). *Gamestorming: A playbook for innovators, rulebreakers, and changemakers*. Sebastopol, CA: O'Reilly.

Higgins (2005). *101 Creative problem solving techniques: The handbook of new ideas for business (revised edition)*. Winter Park, FL: New Management Publishing Company.

Michalko, M. (2006). *Thinkpak: A brainstorming card deck (revised edition)*. Berkeley, CA: Ten Speed Press.

12. **Plan how you will record, track, and decide which brainstorming items to pursue further.** In most cases, you will probably enter the ideas into a spreadsheet or database for later use. A common complaint from brainstorming participants is that they often don't know how the ideas were eventually used. Keep in mind that ideas from one session might be useful a year or more later. You might consider keeping an online catalog of ideas that are searchable or an "idea book" where you organize ideas that might be reusable.

1.3.2 Conducting a Brainstorming Session

1. **Schedule time before the brainstorming session to prepare the room.**
    a. Arrive early to assess the brainstorming facilities. Check whether you have enough tables and chairs and that they can be moved around.
    b. Make sure you have paper, tape, sticky notes, markers, and other materials ready during the session. If you have to fumble with materials during the session, then you are wasting time and blocking the production of ideas by others. A subtle quality of good brainstorming is that of "smooth flow" where disruptive actions (like taking a few minutes to tape more papers on the wall) are minimized.
    c. Tape paper to the wall and have extra sheets ready for the ideas.
    d. Set up remote connections if you have distant participants. Remote brainstorming requires somewhat different rules as it is harder to know when remote participants want to contribute an idea.

e. Arrange the seats so everyone can see the ideas that are generated. If you are going to an unfamiliar location for brainstorming, it is worthwhile asking for a diagram of the room early so you can plan the best layout for the session.

f. Spread snacks around the room to increase the energy level and show that you care for your participants. One snack tip— consider bringing some healthy snacks like carrots, grapes, and celery. A minor, but common gripe at ideation sessions is the lack of low calorie, healthy food.

Ideas for Getting Input from Remote Participants

Many companies are using Internet collaboration tools to conduct business and exchange ideas with geographically dispersed teams. Remote brainstorming using these tools is difficult because it is hard to know when someone at a different site has an idea to contribute. Several possibilities for engaging remote participants include:

- Using electronic brainstorming tools with the remote meeting tool so your distant colleagues can see all the ideas.
- Asking remote participants to type their ideas into chat windows where they can be read off to everyone and added to a physical or electronic list of ideas. You could have someone assigned to type the local ideas into chat so the remote colleagues can have the benefit of seeing as well as hearing all the items.
- Instituting a rule for switching to a remote site and getting their input periodically. For example, you could explicitly ask your remote colleagues to list ideas on paper and then about every 3 minutes or so ask for their ideas to ensure that they aren't forgotten. The problem with explicit switching between the local and remote sites is that you will lose some time (and thus ideas) because of the lag between asking for remote input and getting feedback.

---

2. **Introduce the facilitator and ask the participants to introduce themselves if they do not know each other.** Introductions are important and you might want to do something creative for the introductions, but don't let them drag on too long or allow people to talk past your general guideline—say 1 minute per person. You could make the introductions into a warm-up exercise as noted earlier in this chapter.

3. **Describe the topic of interest and how long the session will last.**
   Display the topic or question for the session prominently by writing it in large clear text on a board or poster (or computer projection) so that it is visible to all participants. This is important for keeping the meeting focused. Focus on one major topic or one aspect of a problem at a time. Nijstad, Diehl, and Stroebe (2003) recommend breaking large problems or topics into several pieces to keep the level of productivity high throughout the session. The introduction of new pieces of a problem or a new topic will lead to increased motivation and idea generation, and will postpone the feeling that ideas have run out.
4. **Include short breaks (5−10 minutes) during a brainstorming session to stimulate different approaches to a problem or to overcome mental blocks.** Schedule short breaks every 20−30 minutes if you have a long brainstorming session or multiple topics to cover. Brainstorming is intense activity and short breaks will keep the ideas flowing. Give the participants cards or sticky notes to write down any thoughts they have during the breaks.
5. **Describe brainstorming to the group and explain the key principles and ground rules of your brainstorming session.** Write these principles and other ground rules on the board or create a playful poster or handout as a constant reminder about what will make the session successful. One of your rules could be that you will explicitly note when someone breaks a rule ("John, you are telling a war story"). Some specific principles that you need to point out every time you conduct a brainstorming session include:
   a. **No criticism, praise, or discussion of any ideas (other than to explain something like an acronym or unfamiliar idea or phrase).** This can include verbal disparagement ("what a dumb idea!") or nonverbal behaviors (facial expressions or body language that indicate disapproval). While most organizers of brainstorming sessions stress the cardinal rule of "no criticism," it is important that the facilitator be aware of subtle verbal and nonverbal behaviors as well as blatant attempts to criticize participants. Keep in mind that "praising" one idea is subtle criticism of "un-praised" ideas.
   b. **Quantity is the sole measure of brainstorming effectiveness.** Stress that the only metric for brainstorming is the sheer number of ideas that the group can generate and anything that gets in the way of quantity is bad.

   c. **Ideas can be totally new, modifications of existing ideas, or ideas that come from combining other ideas.** Explain that there is no shame in expressing an idea that is an extension or modification of another idea or combinations of several ideas. If you were brainstorming breakfast foods your participants might come up with "pancakes" and "eggs" which could be combined into a "pankegg"—an egg cooked inside a pancake (which, by the way, is quite a tasty breakfast item).

6. **Describe what you will do with the brainstorming items that the group decides to examine further.** Failure to inform people about how the ideas will be used may lead to skepticism about the value of brainstorming.

7. **Designate one or more notetakers for the brainstorming session.** For many sessions, the facilitator can write the ideas on the work surface. For longer (and larger) sessions, you might consider several notetakers who alternate recording the ideas so writing delays don't interfere with the brainstorming. If you have two notetakers, one person could write the items on a board or easel while the other writes them on sticky notes for later grouping and prioritization. If you use several notetakers, work out the basic rules for who writes what, when. For example, one rule could be to divide the room or table where people are sitting into two areas and have each notetaker write down the ideas on sticky notes from one side of the table.

The act of recording ideas during brainstorming is essential, but must be done in a way that does not disrupt the flow of ideas. If ideas are flowing quickly, a person who is a sluggish writer will slow the brainstorming down and reduce the quantity of ideas. So, in your planning, consider how to you can capture ideas efficiently and accurately.

Here are some suggestions about how to make the capture of ideas efficient:

- Choose someone with domain knowledge so he or she is familiar with the terminology that the group will use and won't have to ask clarification questions too often.
- Choose a notetaker who is a fast typist or writer.
- Consider using two notetakers with simple rules for who takes what notes.
- Have enough materials at hand for writing and recording. For example, if your notetaker is writing on sticky notes, then have an ample supply of notes and extra markers nearby (How many

of us have been in a meeting where there are brilliant ideas flowing and suddenly the facilitator's marker dries up and there is silence while everyone looks for a good marker).

8. **Describe what you will do with the brainstorming items that the group decides to examine further.** Failure to inform people about how the ideas will be used may lead to skepticism about the value of brainstorming.

9. **Consider a warm-up for your brainstorming.** This warm-up could be a short practice run on a fun topic that you do just before your planned brainstorming session. This warm-up should take only a few minutes but can help loosen inhibitions and put participants in a positive mood. Positive moods have been linked to increases in individual creativity (Grawitch, Munz, Elliott, & Mathis, 2003; Isen, 2000) so taking some time to set up the brainstorming session as a positive, fun, and creative activity is a worthwhile investment. Spreading small plates of candy, grapes, or nuts on the table could be part of your mood enhancement plan.

10. **Review the topic, problem, or question that is the focus of the brainstorming session and remind participants of the brainstorming rules.** Let the participants know that if they violate the rules the facilitator will provide gentle reminders. Ask if there are any questions and if not, begin the brainstorming.

Competitive Brainstorming Can Increase the Quantity of Ideas

Paulus and Dzindolet (1993) conducted a study where participants were given goals that were about twice those of a "typical performance." The groups given high goals increased their performance by about 40%. In addition to setting specific goals, you can urge people to get to the next level by exhorting participants with statements like "we have 90 ideas, let's try for 100 or more!" If you are doing electronic brainstorming you could indicate the average number of ideas being generated per person (although never identify anyone by name). As a general rule, the expectations for group performance should be set reasonably high (Paulus & Brown, 2003).

---

11. **Invite participants to shout their ideas so that everyone can hear, one idea at a time, as quickly as possible.** Do not let participants:
    • Interrupt one another.

- Start elaborating on ideas beyond what is needed to understand the ideas.
- Engage in distracting side conversations, phone calls, texting, or other activities.
- Worry about quality.

What Do You Do When the Rate of Idea Generation Slows Down?

During a brainstorming session, the rate at which ideas are generated will vary from fast and furious to slow and awkward. If there is a lull, take a short break or try a different approach. For example, the facilitator might focus on one idea and ask for variations on it rather than press for completely new ideas. Facilitators can also try using analogies, random words, or other creativity techniques to stimulate some additional ideas (Higgins, 1994; Infinite Innovations, Ltd., n.d.).

---

12. **Ensure that each idea is understood and adequately captured before accepting the next idea.** Allow for brief questions to clarify ideas, terminology, abbreviations, or anything that might not be understood by every participant.
13. **Review the items with the group.** At the end of a session, clarify any unclear or ambiguous items so you will know what each item means even days or weeks later.
14. **Combine duplicate items into a single item.** As noted earlier in this chapter, having duplicate ideas is not a problem—simply combine them into a single item.

1.3.3 After the Brainstorming Session

1. **Designate a specific person or team to handle all the data after the session.**

    Capture all the ideas and record which ones will be considered further. Catalog the ideas, preferably in a database that is easily accessible. Ideas that were not considered important at first may become important later. Your ideas could be useful 2 years from now or help another group who had a similar problem with a different product.

Information Networks to Keep Ideas Alive

Ideas and hunches come from brainstorming and many other sources. Johnson (2010), in his brilliant book, *Where Good Ideas Come From: The Natural History of Innovation*, advocates an open information network that keeps good ideas around and visible to anyone in an organization. Johnson believes that the key to innovation is to keep ideas visible and "liquid" so they can easily be combined, expanded, and modified by everyone. So think about ways to capture your ideas from brainstorming, hallway conversations, meetings, and other activities and make them visible to others. Perhaps ideas could be posted on large monitors in hallways and pulled up from old meetings from the idea database. You might find that the next big idea comes from an idea from an old brainstorming session and a hunch that you had at lunch. You could use tablets as "idea catchers" and "idea labs" that keep ideas alive and banging together until something special emerges.

Tip

If you have a lot of ideas, use a quick method to eliminate the weakest ideas before you use voting, rankings, or ratings. You might, for example, ask the team to sort items into a pile that merits further consideration and a pile that doesn't merit further action. Then you can take the ideas in the "further consideration" pile and reduce those to the best ideas through a rating or ranking process.

2. **Develop a plan for investigating the important items in more detail.** You might, for example, create a matrix of potential solutions, look at the costs and benefits of each, and then narrow the list of ideas to the ones that seem feasible under your current constraints. Some of the general approaches for making decisions about what ideas or solutions to consider further are (Borchers, 1999):
   - **Private rankings or ratings.** Participants in the brainstorming session privately rate the brainstorming items and the highest rated items are considered further. You might, for example, rate each idea on a simple 1 (low priority) to 3 (high priority) scale and then take the average value of the ratings for each idea. You could choose the top 10 for further consideration. Private ratings are at the core of the nominal group technique,

the Delphi method, and other brainstorming variations. Private rankings or ratings are useful for mitigating the influence of managers and loud, influential, domineering, or high-status colleagues.

- **Majority vote.** Participants vote on which ideas to consider and the majority rules. Majority voting can be unwieldy if you have many dozens or hundreds of items.
- **Consensus.** Consensus is an accord reached by a group as a whole. The brainstorming participants or the people designated to choose ideas must all agree on the best ideas through discussion and debate. Achieving true consensus on what ideas to consider can be difficult and requires time outside the actual brainstorming session.
- **Compromise.** Participants come to agreement about what ideas to consider further by giving up some of their individual demands.
- **Decision by a leader.** The final decision is made by a designated leader (who may or may not be the facilitator or one of the participants in the session). For example, the engineering manager who controls the development resources and has to make other trade-offs of time, features, and quality could make the final decision. At some companies, the product managers, who often define the requirements for products, might decide what ideas should be considered further.
- **Arbitration.** Another person or group makes a decision for the brainstorming participants. For example, a usability team might brainstorm solutions for a user interface problem surfaced by developers, but the development manager and product managers would be the final arbiters and make the final decision about which solutions to consider.
- **Criteria-based prioritization.** This is discussed in the data analysis section, but briefly, this approach would rate each idea against explicit criteria like feasibility, cost, and time. The highest rated items across the criteria are chosen for further consideration. Criteria-based prioritization can be hard if you have a large number of items so some way to reduce the number of ideas to a manageable size first is recommended.

3. **Consider a method for tracking which ideas are used during product development.** Assign ownership and due dates to the chosen ideas

and solutions so there is a clear assignment of responsibility for developing possible ideas and solutions.

4. **Collect feedback on the brainstorming.** You might ask participants to fill out a short survey or you might conduct a short "plus/delta" session where everyone is asked to discuss what worked well (the "plusses") and what could work better (the "deltas"). Apply good suggestions to future brainstorming sessions.

1.4 VARIATIONS AND EXTENSIONS TO BRAINSTORMING

1.4.1 Buzz Sessions (Also Known as the Philips 66 Technique)

The buzz session, or Philips 66 technique, is a way to generate ideas when you have groups that are too large for traditional brainstorming, like a college class or a group of colleagues at a professional conference. The buzz session divides a large group (say more than 12 people) into several smaller groups (4–6 people). The small groups are given a topic, a brief set of rules, and then asked to brainstorm for a period of time (6 people for 6 min in the Philips 66 technique). At the end of 6 minutes, the groups report on the results of their brainstorming (or other activity like prioritizing ideas). The idea here is that you might have a large group for a short period of time that could provide valuable input to a question or problem. The major benefit of this brainstorming variation is that it gives more people a chance to speak. A major disadvantage is that you have to coordinate multiple groups and decide how to report and combine the results (Brahm & Kleiner, 1996). You might also have some initial inertia to overcome if the people in the short-lived groups don't know each other.

1.4.2 Free Listing

Free listing is a fast way to get ideas on a topic or possible answers to a question. Free listing (Sinha, 2003) involves asking individual participants or a group to list as many ideas as possible on a specific topic in a short period of time, often just a few minutes.

Some examples of free listing questions for user-centered design are:

- List all the ideas you have for solving (description of a problem).
- List all the tasks that you perform in the course of a week.
- List all the tools that you use in your work.
- List all the forms and documents that you use in your work.

- List all the functions that you use in (put product name here).
- List all the things about (put product name here) that frustrate or irritate you.

Free listing is a research technique used by cognitive anthropologists to uncover how different cultural groups classify concepts (Bernard, 2006). For example, you might ask members of a particular cultural group to, "List all the foods they eat." Trotter (1981) first asked 378 Mexican Americans what home remedies for illnesses they knew and then what illness was treated by which remedy. From these two questions, he was able to compare response frequencies by gender, age, place of birth, and other factors. The results of free listing can be used to rank order the words or phrases by frequency or other dimensions (Bernard, 2006; Hines, 1993).

Free listing can be used to understand terminology, concepts, behaviors, and beliefs. In the domain of user-centered design, free listing can be used to gather ideas and complement brainstorming and other idea generation methods. However, you can also use free listing as cultural anthropologists do, to understand cultural and cognitive domains of users and other stakeholders. Sinha (2003) recommends free listing as a method for understanding a domain or mental model by examining the frequency and order of answers to the free listing question. If there is statistical consistency across participants in the frequency and position of many items in a list, the researcher would have a "coherent domain"; if there is little consistency in the set of free listing items, the domain may not be too coherent.

Tip

You can use free listing as a way to get ideas from a very large group in a short time or as a warm-up exercise for group brainstorming.

Free listing questions can be asked in questionnaires, during individual or group interviews, in focus groups, in e-mail, listservs, wikis, and other online techniques. If you are using this information to study a particular group, you may want to conduct face-to-face free listing so you can use probes to increase recall (Bernard, 2006). Brewer, Garrett, and Rinaldi (2002) compared two types of probes for increasing the number of items in a list:

1. **Alphabetic probes** in which you ask participants after a free listing activity if they knew any more items starting with successive letters of the alphabet. So after a person does a free listing about usability methods, you might say "Think of all the usability or user-centered methods that begin with the letter 'A' and tell me any new ones that you haven't already said." This might prompt a person to remember "affinity diagramming" and "A/B Testing." You would do this for each letter in the alphabet.

2. **Semantic probes** in which you instruct the participant to go through the list generated earlier and use those items as cues for additional ones. Here you would ask something like "Try to remember usability or user-centered design methods that are similar to [the first item listed by the participants]." For example, if a person had listed "heuristic evaluation," you could ask "Are there any other methods that are like a heuristic evaluation?" to which the person might remember that she had once used a "structured heuristic walkthrough." You would do this for each item in the original list. Brewer and his colleagues found that semantic cues were somewhat more effective than alphabetic cues for generating new items.

The benefits of free listing are:

- It is simple, but powerful.
- You can administer the free listing method to large groups as well as individual participants.
- Free listing can be done face to face or remotely using the phone and a variety of electronic methods like chat or wikis.
- It is a quick way to gather information about a domain, product, or process.

The drawbacks of free listing are:

- Participants may forget items.
- Participants may not understand that they should generate an exhaustive list, though good instructions can help.

- Answers may require some interpretation. For example, if you asked participants to list all the attributes that they associated with user-friendly products, they might combine two separate attributes in a compound phrase ("quick and easy to learn"). You might also have people use idiosyncratic phrases that require interpretation like "a kernel that keeps on goin" or close synonyms like "credible" and "trustworthy" where you might have to decide if they were similar enough to be a single item.
- The basic data analysis is simple, but it can also get complex and involve cluster analysis, multidimensional scaling, and other sophisticated analyses.

1.4.3 The Nominal Group Technique

The nominal group technique (Delbecq, Van deVen, & Gustafson, 1975; Higgins, 1994; McGraw & Harbison, 1997; Stasser & Birchmeier, 2003; VanGundy, 1984) is designed to reduce the social anxiety associated with face-to-face group brainstorming. In the nominal group technique, participants are given a problem or topic and asked to write ideas privately for a specified period of time. Then all the ideas are listed on a board by having each participant read out one idea at a time. If a participant doesn't have an idea, he or she can pass for that round. No criticism is allowed when the ideas are read out. When all ideas are listed publicly, the facilitator reviews each idea to see if any further clarification is needed. If so, the person who proposed the idea has 10−30 seconds to explain (but not defend, refute, or sell) the idea.

After everyone understands all the ideas, the participants vote on the ideas using a secret ballot. If you are going to vote right after brainstorming, you can put numbers on each idea and hand people a "ballot" with corresponding numbers and ask them to vote for a number (say 10 or 20) of ideas that they think warrant consideration. The ballots are anonymous—no names are associated with the votes. The votes are tabulated during a break and the ideas with the most votes or highest average ranks are chosen for further consideration. If there are too many ideas after the first voting session, a second round of voting can be conducted.

Using Anonymous Idea Cards in the Nominal Group Technique

To reduce the anxiety of participants in the nominal group technique even further, you could present the topic or question and then ask everyone to spend a few minutes writing ideas on 3 × 5 cards or sticky notes—one idea per card or note (Teaching Effectiveness Program, n.d.). When time is up, you can collect the cards and then redistribute them randomly to the group. Then ask participants to read aloud what is on each card as they place them on a large table or stick them to a wall. Participants can ask for clarification on the items. Then you can conduct the secret ballot on the ideas. This approach separates people from ideas and is meant to reduce the anxiety associated with the creation of ideas and voting on the best ideas.

The benefits of the nominal group technique are:

- A reduction of the social inhibitions and anxieties that might occur in traditional brainstorming.
- A highly efficient method for generating ideas.
- A better chance for equal participation because quiet, shy, or fearful participants have a chance to state their ideas.
- A separation of ideas from personalities of the originators (especially if you use the anonymous card approach mentioned above).
- A reduction in the evaluation apprehension that group members may feel if there are status differences among the participants (e.g., your boss or vice president is in the group).
- A sense of closure since private voting is a specific step in the procedure (it may or may not be in traditional group brainstorming).

The drawbacks of the nominal group technique are:

- Limited interaction among the group members.
- The relative obscurity of the method. It is not a well-known variation on traditional group brainstorming.
- A lack of synergy because all ideas are generated privately.
- A possible lack of convergence on what the best ideas are during the prioritization or voting (e.g., many ideas each get a few votes with no clear "winner").

For details on how to conduct a nominal group session, see *Group Techniques for Program Planning: A Guide to Nominal Group and Delphi Processes* (Delbecq et al., 1975).

Table 1.2 Negative Items from Reverse Brainstorming and Their Positive Counterparts	
Topic: What Can We Do to Make Our Customers Dissatisfied?	
Negative Statements	**Positive Statements**
• Keep people from returning items—it is real expensive • Hide the link for returns to the company	• Highlight the liberal return policy in a clear block above the fold • Put the link at the top of the page for returns
• Avoid telling customers how much shipping is for their orders	• Provide an estimator for shipping before customers have to fill out a lot of information • Provide rough estimates in a table that shows the various ways to ship
• Hide the phone number for calling our company directly • "Virtual" companies should not tell people where they are located or how to call	• Provide a customer support phone number in the contacts area and also during checkout
• Do not tell people that their passwords are case sensitive. • Do not make it easy to retrieve passwords • Do not warn people that their password is insecure	• Provide a short tip on password formats • Ignore case (but require at least one number) • Provide an easy way to retrieve lost passwords

1.4.4 Reverse (Negative) Brainstorming

This is a variation on brainstorming where you ask participants to first brainstorm negative aspects of a topic and then, with the list of negative aspects visible, brainstorm positive items for related clusters of comments. (CreatingMinds.org, n.d.; MindTools, n.d.; VanGundy, 1984).

The basic procedure for reverse brainstorming is to:

1. **Brainstorm on a negative topic.** For example, instead of asking "How can we improve customer satisfaction?" you might ask "What can we do to make customers dissatisfied?" or "How can we cause customers to be dissatisfied?" or "How can we make customers mad?" You could also ask "What is everyone else NOT doing?" rather than list what they are doing to improve product satisfaction.

2. **Group related comments.** Arrange related items in groups to simplify the next step.

3. **Generate positive statements for the negative groups of items.** In Table 1.2, negative statements about customer support for an e-commerce site are listed in the left column and positive statements on the right.

4. **Evaluate the positive statements for potential solutions.**

The philosophy behind reverse brainstorming is that it is easier to find fault first, then use the faults as input on how to improve some aspect of a product or service. You might also use this approach when:

- You have a very judgmental group and traditional group brainstorming is difficult.
- You are working on a product or service that is complex to implement (Mycoted, 2006).

1.4.5 Delphi Method

The Delphi method was developed at the RAND research institute in the 1960s (Brown, 1968) to study the opinions of experts without having face-to-face meetings where psychological factors such as dominant personalities, status, or approval could strongly influence the outcome of the meetings.

Weblink

To learn more about RAND and the original Delphi method, see www.rand.org.

The Delphi method involves a coordinator and a group of experts who are given a problem and a questionnaire that asks for ideas about how to solve the problem, and general questions related to the problem (Delbecq et al., 1975). The experts provide reasons for their opinions which are then critiqued by the rest of the experts. After they fill out the initial questionnaire, the results are collated and summarized by the coordinator and sent back to the panel of experts with no names attached to the ideas. A second questionnaire asks more specific questions (based on the earlier results) and once again the anonymous results are sent around to the experts who evaluate the ideas from the second round and add any new ideas.

The coordinator repeats the process of summarizing the results and sending out new questionnaires until there is convergence on the best ideas for solving the problem. The selection of the best ideas can emerge as a result of consensus of the experts, or the final set of ideas can be ranked or rated anonymously. The Delphi method is most often applied to complex problems with relatively large groups of experts.

Given the complexity of modern software development where requirements must be multinational and design is done by multiple groups across many time zones, the Delphi method has a place in the repertoire of user-centered professionals.

Delphi Studies by E-mail

Early Delphi studies relied on traditional paper mail. The exchange of questionnaires and responses between the coordinator and the team of experts could consume many weeks. The Delphi method is powerful, but coordinators can spend many hours creating the succession of questionnaires and feedback forms necessary for converging on the best ideas. With e-mail, chat, and wiki software, this delay can be reduced considerably.

For current examples of the use of Delphi method, see Harrison, Back, and Tatar (2006) who employed a version of the Delphi method for project planning of design projects and Francis, Firth, and Mellor (2005) who used the Delphi method to examine user-centered design of assistive technologies with autistic users.

1.4.6 Remote Brainstorming

Remote brainstorming can be accomplished with synchronous (e.g., chat) and asynchronous (e.g., blogs, wikis, and other social media) communication technologies. Here are some general approaches for remote brainstorming:

- **E-mail.** Participants can do individual brainstorming and send items to an e-mail address where they are combined and then listed on a web site or other type of archive.
- **Listserv software.** Remote participants can submit ideas that are circulated to everyone on the brainstorming team. The facilitator compiles the items and makes them available to the group for prioritization or further review.
- **Online chat and instant messaging.** You can assemble a distributed team to brainstorm topics using chat or instant messaging software. Members of the brainstorming team are sent instructions beforehand with the topic of interest and rules for the session. The session is recorded and the ideas that are generated can be prioritized later. One of the problems with using chat or instant messaging is that

ideas can scroll out of view so you lose the ability to see everything, which is important for encouraging variations on ideas that were listed earlier.

- **Electronic whiteboards.** Electronic whiteboards allow distributed teams to post ideas in during a brainstorming session. You can use whiteboards and conference calling systems to run remote brainstorming sessions.

Tip

The first time you use a remote approach for brainstorming, conduct a pilot test with a small group of remote participants to work out technical issues, ground rules, and best practices.

- **Blogs and wikis.** Remote participants can add comments on a specific topic or question to a blog or wiki for a designated period of time.
- **Google spreadsheet.** Google spreadsheet is an efficient tool for conducting remote brainstorming sessions. You can assign individuals or teams at remote sites to a column in a Google spreadsheet and then have each person or group enter items into the column. As the items are entered, they appear in everyone's spreadsheet.
- **Specialized online brainstorming software.** A search of the Web using search phrases like "online brainstorming" or "brainstorming software" will reveal commercial online brainstorming tools and services with specialized features like threaded idea generation, features for organizing ideas, facilitator prompts, polls for rating ideas, and decision matrices where each idea is rated against a set of criteria.
- **Visual diagramming and mind mapping software.** Some visual diagramming and mind mapping software can be used for brainstorming. Examples are Inspiration, MindMeister, and Mindjet MindManager.

Dennis and Williams (2003) compared electronic brainstorming to verbal (face-to-face) brainstorming and nominal brainstorming where people worked in the presence of each other but did not share ideas verbally or in writing. Their research revealed that electronic brainstorming can be an efficient complement to verbal or nominal group brainstorming especially for large groups.

1.5 MAJOR ISSUES IN THE USE OF BRAINSTORMING

1.5.1 What Is "Quality" in Brainstorming?

A mantra of brainstorming is that quantity begets quality, but just what is this "quality"? Quality in brainstorming research is generally measured by considering the novelty or originality of an idea and the feasibility or appropriateness of the idea to the problem at hand. So a quality idea might be considered as something that others haven't thought of before that can be reasonably implemented with the resources available. One way to examine the quality of ideas from brainstorming sessions is to have several experts rate ideas for their novelty and appropriateness. Other criteria used in research to evaluate the outcomes of brainstorming sessions include (Isaksen, 1998):

- Satisfaction with the ideas generated
- Flexibility of the ideas
- Generality of the ideas.

The often-repeated statement that quality comes from quantity is generally supported in the research literature. Diehl and Stroebe (1987), for example, found a high correlation ($r = 0.82$) between the quantity of ideas generated and the number of "quality" ideas.

One open issue with regard to the value of brainstorming is the overall impact of good brainstorming ideas on product success. What is the return on investment (ROI) associated with brainstorming and the ideas that are applied from the brainstorming? There doesn't seem to be a good answer for that yet.

1.5.2 How Many Participants Should I Have in Brainstorming Sessions?

Earlier in this chapter, the recommended number of participants for effective group brainstorming ranged from three to ten people with some diversity in background. The optimal size of a group is determined, in part, by factors that influence production gains (larger groups may have more synergy and more persistence) and production losses (social anxiety, evaluation apprehension, production blocking, and cognitive interference where old ideas start popping up and people have to think if the idea is new or old). Diversity, for example, can result in idea production gains, but also result in losses if the diverse participants use a different language or have a different perspective that results in communication problems (Nijstad, Diehl, & Stroebe, 2003).

There are many variables to consider when assessing what size brainstorming groups should be in a particular context, but there is a general trend in the research literature favoring relatively small groups of three to six participants. Heller and Hollabaugh (1992), for example, recommend small groups that do not exceed three people. In the real world, there is also a larger organizational issue that brainstorming with a small group may be seen as relegating the nonparticipants to an "outgroup" and engender some hostility in those who were not invited. So, for practical use, somewhere between three and ten people is reasonable and you can always run two medium-sized groups.

1.5.3 Social Issues that could Affect Idea Generation in Group Brainstorming

Brainstorming involves a number of social issues that can impair creativity (Paulus & Nijstad, 2003). These social issues include:

- **Fear of evaluation by other members of the group.** Evaluation apprehension, the fear or being evaluated or tested, is a serious issue for group brainstorming (Camacho & Paulus, 1995; Rosenberg, 1969). Participants may not want to put forth wild ideas if they are afraid of losing credibility, having their idea rejected, or being humiliated. Facilitators can reduce evaluation apprehension by:
  - Not inviting someone that the group fears. Avoid inviting managers who are tyrannical or several levels above most of the other participants. This is not the time to invite the CEO to drop by.
  - Stressing that the quantity of ideas is the sole criterion for brainstorming success.
  - Reminding participants that all ideas are welcome.
  - Pointing out that the participants will not be judged on the quality of ideas. The worst thing that any facilitator or manager can do to stifle brainstorming would be to hint (or publically state) that the results of brainstorming will be used as input to employees' performance reviews.
- **Competition for speaking time.** Facilitators should encourage participants to:
  - Respond crisply.
  - Not belabor an idea once it is understood.

- Avoid criticism.
- Watch for cues that someone is struggling to get his or her ideas out. While everyone should have a chance to speak, forcing people to speak or "going around the table" for input from everyone is generally not recommended. Putting people on the spot can be terrifying.

- **Listening to others.** A common (and often ignored) rule in brainstorming is that only one person speaks at a time. Some brainstorming researchers and practitioners even recommend that participants raise their hands if they have an idea to avoid interrupting a person who is currently expressing an idea. However, requiring participants to raise their hands may seem too juvenile for many professional offices.
- **No side conversations.** A primary responsibility of the facilitator is to suppress side conversations because they will distract the group and block the production of new ideas.
- **Avoid "filler conversations".** Filler conversations occur when a participant states an idea and then goes on to explain or elaborate excessively on the idea or "tells a war story." Filler wastes time that could be used to generate new ideas and can block the production of ideas by others who have to listen. Group brainstorming is more effective when filler material is kept to a minimum (Dugosh, Paulus, Roland, & Yang, 2000).

1.6 DATA ANALYSIS

1.6.1 Types of Data

Types of data that can be collected during brainstorming include:

- A list of ideas generated by the participants.
- Groupings of ideas into categories at the end of brainstorming sessions using the affinity diagramming method.
- Elaborations and explanations of ideas during review.
- A list of prioritized ideas.
- Ratings of the ideas on one or more criteria.
- Feedback about the brainstorming process itself.

1.6.2 Analysis Techniques

1.6.2.1 Listing Ideas

All the ideas from a brainstorming session can be listed in a spreadsheet, database, word processor, or specialized tools like PathMaker®

or Inspiration. If you have numbered the items sequentially as they were generated, your list would be chronological. To facilitate recall days, weeks, or even months later when you look through this list, you can annotate the list with clarifications and brief explanation of any unusual terms or abbreviations.

1.6.2.2 Affinity Diagramming—Grouping Ideas from Brainstorming

Affinity diagramming is a method for organizing qualitative data into related groups. For example, you could extract behavioral statements or other units of data from a series of field interviews, focus groups, or usability testing and then have your product team and other stakeholders organize the statements into related groups (Figure 1.1). These groups are then broken down into subgroups (and if you have large amounts of data, sub-subgroups). After creating a hierarchy of related information, the groups and their subgroups are given names. Affinity diagramming is often used to organize data from field studies, contextual inquiry, brainstorming, diary studies, usability testing, and other methods that generate qualitative data.

The affinity diagramming method originated with the software quality movement that began in Japan (Babbar, Behara, & White, 2002). The original intent of the affinity diagramming was to help

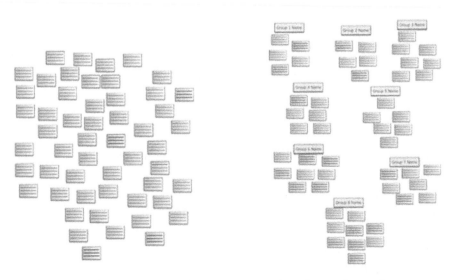

Figure 1.1 Ungrouped data before an affinity diagramming session and named groups after a session.

diagnose complex problems by organizing data from various sources to reveal themes related to the problem. The basic affinity diagramming method involves:

1. Gathering qualitative data from multiple stakeholders. This data can be text or images or work artifacts.
2. Writing units of data on "sticky notes," note cards, or even magnetic "paper".
3. Placing the items on a large surface.
4. Asking the participants to organize the items into "affinity groups"—groups of items that "go together" or that are related in some way (Figure 1.1).
5. Breaking large groups of notes into smaller subgroups.
6. Asking the participants to generate names (often called "labels") for the affinity groups and subgroups.
7. "Walking the diagram" as a group to ensure that everyone is clear on the meaning of the items and names for the groups.
8. Drawing the diagram formed by the groups and subgroups. The part of the process is used to clearly show the relationships between groups.
9. Prioritizing the items for further consideration in the design of products or processes.

1.6.2.3 Voting on Brainstorming Ideas
A group can vote on which brainstorming items should be considered further by placing adhesive dots or ink marks on items, by removing items from the master list, or voting online using tools like Excel, Google Spreadsheet, or SurveyMonkey.

1.6.2.4 Criteria-Based Evaluation
Criteria-based evaluation uses a decision matrix to choose the top ideas from brainstorming. The people charged with choosing which ideas will be considered further rate or rank each idea against a list of criteria like cost, ease of programming, novelty, and generality. The ratings or rankings for each idea are averaged, the ideas sorted by the average value, and the top rated or ranked ideas chosen for consideration. Criteria-based evaluation can be done with online survey tools if you want to expand the choice of top ideas beyond the original brainstorming participants (Table 1.3).

Table 1.3 A Decision Matrix for a Criterion-Based Approach to Choosing the Best Ideas from Brainstorming							
	Criterion 1	Criterion 2	Criterion 3	...	Criterion N	Sum	Mean Rating/ Ranking	Top Ideas
Idea 1								
Idea 2								
Idea 3								
Idea 4								
Idea	...	...	...	...	...	...	...	
Idea N								

1.7 WHAT DO YOU NEED FOR BRAINSTORMING?

1.7.1 Personnel, Participants, and Training

You need a small, diverse group of three to ten people for a brainstorming session and a facilitator who will explain the process and keep the session going efficiently. An experienced facilitator is important for successful brainstorming. Key attributes of a good facilitator for brainstorming would include:

- An ability to keep participants from engaging in critical analysis of ideas too soon.
- Sufficient energy to keep ideas flowing.
- A focus on the quantity of ideas rather than the quality (quality assessment comes later).
- Acceptance of radical ideas.

Training requirements for the brainstorming facilitator are moderate. Research into methods for generating ideas (Paulus & Brown, 2003) highlights the need for experienced facilitators who are trained in procedures for effective group interaction (Paulus & Brown, 2003). Facilitators should be trained to:

- Apply the brainstorming rules consistently.
- Motivate participants using a variety of prompts.
- Ensure that no one dominates the session.
- Keep the focus on one issue, question, or topic, at a time.
- Notice when people are becoming fatigued.
- Be aware of best practices for ensuring effective group interaction.

- Deal with the occasional silent period. Sometimes participants will need to think a bit so the facilitator should not panic at momentary lulls in the conversation.

Training requirements for participants are relatively low. A short introduction to the brainstorming method and a clear statement of the rules are basic requirements. The most difficult training issues for participants are probably those of minimizing verbal and nonverbal criticism and keeping filler conversations and war stories to a minimum. Smith (1993) found that groups with just 5 minutes of training on the effects of criticism of ideas produced more ideas than groups with no training. Examples of verbal criticism and other behaviors that will result in production blocking and fewer ideas should be a standard part of training for brainstorming.

1.7.2 Hardware and Software
No special hardware of software is required for brainstorming. Brainstorming can be done by writing ideas on a board or using sticky notes that you can affix to a board, wall, or other large surface. If you plan to organize ideas, using sticky notes makes grouping simple but may slow down the brainstorming (you may want two notetakers to write down items). You could also have someone type in ideas on a computer and project them to the brainstorming group (this is useful for remote brainstorming with distributed groups).

You can use software like Word and Excel to capture ideas from brainstorming sessions, but these business applications make it somewhat hard to move items around quickly and easily. Software tools like Inspiration and MindManager can be used to capture ideas quickly and then move and categorize those ideas.

1.7.3 Documents and Materials
The key documents for group brainstorming include:

- A checklist with all the activities that you need to prepare and conduct the brainstorming session.
- A statement of the problem or topic for brainstorming. This statement should be given to all the participants or posted in the location that is visible during the brainstorming session.
- A set of brainstorming ground rules.
- A list of the ideas generated during the session.

- A list of the ideas that are chosen for further consideration (through ratings, rankings, or other forms of prioritization).
- An action statement or plan that describes who is responsible for following up on brainstorming ideas.

The only materials you need for face-to-face group brainstorming are sheets of paper, pens or markers, easels with poster paper, and some way to attach the pages of brainstorming to a wall or other surface that can serve as a temporary idea display.

RECOMMENDED READINGS

Higgins, J. M. (1994). *101 Creative problem solving techniques: The handbook of new ideas for business.* Winter, Park, FL: The New Management Publishing Company. Higgins' book is a compendium of problem-solving techniques. This book describes methods at a high level and provides practitioners who have used some traditional methods like face-to-face group brainstorming with variations for special cases (e.g., very large groups).

Osborn, A. (1963). *Applied imagination: Principles and procedures of creative problem-solving (third revised edition).* New York, NY: Charles Scribner's Sons. This is considered a classic book on modern brainstorming. Alex Osborn, who began his writings on brainstorming in the 1940s, wanted a type of meeting that would reduce the inhibitions that block the generation of creative ideas. Many of the classic rules for modern brainstorming originated with Osborn. This book is out of print, but a worthwhile read if you can locate it. There are a number of versions of this book, each incorporating new ideas from Osborn. The 1963 version is the most-often cited. Used copies are generally available and reprints can be found at http://www.creativeeducationfoundation.org/press.shtml#imagination.

Paulus, P. B., & Nijstad, B. A. (Eds.). (2003). *Group creativity: Innovation through collaboration.* Oxford, UK: Oxford University Press. Paulus and Nijstad have edited a book that captures a wide range of research into group creativity. Much of the book deals with brainstorming and related methods for generating ideas and solutions to problems. While the book is loaded with research and theory, most chapters have a set of practical implications for group creativity methods like brainstorming and brainwriting. The book discusses both face-to-face and electronic methods and their respective strengths and weaknesses. The book highlights how social inhibitors can affect creative productivity and provides some research-based tips on how to overcome these inhibitors.

REFERENCES

Babbar, S., Behara, R., & White, E. (2002). Mapping product usability. *International Journal of Operations and Production Management, 22*(10), 1071–1089.

Berkun, S. *How to run a brainstorming meeting.* (2004). <http://www.scottberkun.com/essays/34-how-to-run-a-brainstorming-meeting/> Accessed 28.10.12.

Bernard, R. H. (2006). *Research methods in anthropology: Qualitative and quantitative approaches* (4th ed.). Lanham, MD: Altamira Press.

Borchers, R. (1999). *Small group communication: Decision-making.* <http://www.abacon.com/commstudies/groups/decision.html> Accessed 21.10.05.

Brahm, C., & Kleiner, B. H. (1996). Advantages and disadvantages of group decision-making approaches. *Team Performance Management: An International Journal, 2*(1), 30–35.

Brewer, D. D., Garrett, S. B., & Rinaldi, G. (2002). Patterns in the recall of sexual and drug injection partners. In J. A. Levy, & B. A. Pescosolido (Eds.), *Social networks and health* (Advances in Medical Sociology, *Volume 8*) (pp. 131–149). Emerald Group Publishing Limited.

Brown, B. B. (1968). *A methodology used for the elicitation of opinions of experts.* Santa Monica, CA: RAND Corporation.

Camacho, M. L., & Paulus, P. B. (1995). The role of social anxiousness in group brainstorming. *Journal of Personality and Social Psychology, 68*(6), 1071–1080.

CreatingMinds.org. *Reverse brainstorming.* (n.d.) <http://creatingminds.org/tools/reverse_brainstorming.htm> Accessed 28.10.12.

Delbecq, A. L., Van deVen, A. H., & Gustafson, D. H. (1975). *Group techniques for program planners.* Glenview, IL: Scott Foresman and Company.

Dennis, A. R., & Williams, M. L. (2003). Electronic brainstorming: Theory, research, and future. In P. B. Paulus, & B. A. Nijstad (Eds.), *Group creativity: Innovation through collaboration* (pp. 160–178). London: Oxford University Press.

Diehl, M., & Stroebe, W. (1987). Productivity loss in brainstorming groups: Toward the solution of a riddle. *Journal of Personality and Social Psychology, 53*, 497–509.

Dugosh, K. L., Paulus, P. B., Roland, E. J., & Yang, H. C. (2000). Cognitive stimulation in brainstorming. *Journal of Personality and Social Psychology, 79*, 722–735.

Francis, P., Firth, L., & Mellor, D. (2005). Reducing the risk of abandonment of assistive technologies for people with autism. In Proceedings of the 2005 IFIP TC13 international conference on Human-Computer Interaction (INTERACT'05), Maria Francesca Costabile and Fabio Paternò (Eds.). Springer-Verlag, Berlin, Heidelberg, 1104–1107.

Freeman, E., & Gelernter, D. (1996). Lifestreams: A storage model for personal data. *SIGMOD Rec., 25*(1), 80–86.

Gray, D., Brown, S., & Macanufo, J. (2010). *Gamestorming: A playbook for innovators, rule-breakers, and changemakers.* Sebastopol, CA: O'Reilly.

Grawitch, M. J., Munz, D. C., Elliott, E. K., & Mathis, A. (2003). Promoting creativity in temporary problem-solving groups: The effects of positive mood and autonomy in problem definition on idea-generating performance. *Group Dynamics: Theory Research, and Practice, 7*(3), 200–213.

Harrison, S., Back, M., & Tatar, D. (2006). "It's just a method!": A pedagogical experiment in interdisciplinary design. In: Proceedings of the sixth ACM conference on designing interactive systems (pp. 261–270). University Park, PA, USA, June 26–28. DIS '06. New York, NY: ACM Press.

Heller, P., & Hollabaugh., M. (1992). Teaching problem solving through cooperative grouping. Pt. 2: Designing problems and structuring groups. *American Journal of Physics, 60*, 637–644.

Higgins, J. M. (2005). *101 creative problem solving techniques: The handbook of new ideas for business* (Revised Edition). Winter Park, FL: New Management Publishing Company.

Hines, A. M. (1993). Linking qualitative and quantitative methods in cross-cultural survey research: Techniques from cognitive science. *American Journal of Community Psychology, 21*, 729–746.

Huseman, R. (1973). The role of the nominal group in small group communication. In R. C. Huseman, D. Logue, & D. Freshley (Eds.), *Readings in interpersonal and organizational communications* (2nd ed.). Boston, MA: Hollbrook.

Infinite Innovations, Ltd. *Creative thinking and lateral thinking techniques.* (n.d.) <http://www.brainstorming.co.uk/tutorials/creativethinkingcontents.html> Accessed 28.10.12.

Isaksen, S. G. (1998). *A review of brainstorming research: Six critical issues for inquiry.* Buffalo, NY: Creative Research Unit, Creative Problem Solving Group-Buffalo.

Isen, A. M. (2000). Positive affect and decision making. In M. Lewis, & J. M. Haviland-Jones (Eds.), *Handbook of emotions* (2nd ed., pp. 417–435). New York, NY: Guildford Press.

Johnson, S. (2010). *Where good ideas come from: The natural history of innovation.* New York, NY: Penguin Books.

Kelley, T. (2001). *The art of innovation: Lessons in creativity from IDEO, America's leading design firm.* New York, NY: Doubleday.

McGraw, K., & Harbison, K. (1997). *User-centered requirements: The scenario-based engineering process.* Mahwah, NJ: Lawrence Erlbaum.

Milliken, F. J., & Martins, L. (1996). Searching for common threads: Understanding the multiple effects of diversity in organizational groups. *Academy of Management Review, 21,* 402–433.

Milliken, F. J., Bartel, C. A., & Kurtzberg, T. R. (2003). Diversity and creativity and work groups: A dynamic perspective on the affective and cognitive processes that link diversity and performance. In P. B. Paulus, & B. A. Nijstad (Eds.), *Group Creativity: Innovation through collaboration* (pp. 32–62). New York, NY: Oxford University Press.

MindTools. *Reverse brainstorming* (n.d.). <http://www.mindtools.com/pages/article/newCT_96.htm> Accessed 28.10.12.

Mycoted. *Negative brainstorming.* (2006) <http://www.mycoted.com/Negative_Brainstorming> Accessed 28.10.12.

Nijstad, B. A., Diehl, M., & Stroebe, W. (2003). Cognitive stimulation and interference in idea generating groups. In P. B. Paulus, & B. A. Nijstad (Eds.), *Group creativity: Innovation through collaboration* (pp. 137–159). New York, NY: Oxford University Press.

OED (Oxford English Dictionary) Online. *Definition of brain-storm.* <www.oed.com>. Accessed 25.10.12.

Osborn, A. F. (1963). *Applied imagination: Principles and procedures of creative problem-solving* (3rd rev. ed.). New York, NY: Charles Scribner's Sons.

Paulus, P. B., & Brown, V. R. (2003). Enhancing ideational creativity in groups: Lessons from research on brainstorming. In P. B. Paulus, & B. A. Nijstad (Eds.), *Group creativity: Innovation through collaboration* (pp. 110–136). Oxford, UK: Oxford University Press.

Paulus, P. B., & Dzindolet, M. T. (1993). Social influence processes in group brainstorming: The illusion of group productivity. *Journal of Personality and Social Psychology, 64,* 575–586.

Rosenberg, M. J. (1969). The conditions and consequences of evaluation apprehension. In R. Rosenthal, & R. L. Rosnow (Eds.), *Artifact in behavioral research* (pp. 279–349). New York, NY: Academic Press.

Sandberg, J. (2006). Brainstorming works best if people scramble for ideas on their own. *The Wall Street Journal,* <http://online.wsj.com/article/SB115015518018078348-email.html> Accessed 25.10.12.

Sinha, R. (2003). Beyond cardsorting: Free-listing methods to explore user categorizations. *Boxes and Arrows,* <http://www.boxesandarrows.com/view/beyond_cardsorting_free_listing_methods_to_explore_user_categorizations> Accessed 28.10.12.

Smith, B. L. (1993). Interpersonal behaviors that damage the productivity of creative problem-solving groups. *Journal of Creative Behavior, 27*(3), 171–187.

Stasser, G., & Birchmeier, Z. (2003). Group creativity and collective choice. In P. B. Paulus, & B. A. Nijstad (Eds.), *Group creativity: Innovation through collaboration* (pp. 85–109). Oxford, UK: Oxford University Press.

Teaching Effectiveness Program. (n.d.). Leading A Discussion Using the Nominal Group Technique. < http://tep.uoregon.edu/services/newsletter/year95-96/issue30/nominal.html/ >. Accessed 13.12.13.

Trotter, R. (1981). Remedioas caseros: Mexican-American home remedies and community health problems. *Social Science and Medicine, 15B,* 107–114.

Trotter, R., & Schensul, J. J. (1998). Methods in applied anthropology. In H. R. Bernard (Ed.), *Handbook of methods in cultural anthropology.* Walnut Creek: CA: AltaMira Press.

Trotter, R., & Schensul, J. J. (2000). Methods in applied anthropology. In H. Russell, & Bernard (Eds.), *Handbook of methods in cultural anthropology* (pp. 691–735). Walnut Creek, CA: AltaMira Press.

Van Gundy, A. B. (1984). *Managing group creativity.* New York, NY: American Management Association.

Wellner, A. S. (2003). *A perfect brainstorm.* Inc. Online, < http://www.inc.com/magazine/20031001/strategies.html/ > Accessed 13.01.13.

CHAPTER 2

Brainwriting

Alternate Names: Brainwriting, cascade session, idea writing, individual brainstorming, non-oral brainstorming.

Related Methods: Affinity diagramming, braindrawing, brainstorming, free listing, nominal group technique (NGT).

2.1 OVERVIEW OF BRAINWRITING

Brainwriting (sometimes called "individual brainstorming") is a method for rapidly generating ideas by asking participants to write their ideas on paper (or online) and exchanging written ideas rather than shouting those ideas out as happens during traditional brainstorming (Brahm & Kleiner, 1996). Table 2.1 is a scorecard that highlights the relative investment needed to conduct a brainwriting session and when brainwriting is most useful.

While brainwriting is less well known than traditional group brainstorming (Osborn, 1963), Paulus and Brown (2003) provided evidence that brainwriting often produces more ideas than group brainstorming. Because each person is writing down ideas at the same time, the process involves parallel activity as compared to brainstorming where only one idea can be "shouted out" at a time. Spreng (2007) noted that when you have four people in a 20-minutes brainstorming session, you are brainstorming for 20 minutes, but if you ask four people to spend 20 minutes each writing down answers (as fast as they can) to a brainwriting question, you really have something more like an 80-minutes brainstorming session.

Brainstorming Versus Brainwriting

Brainwriting is not yet a common technique in user-centerd design (UCD) for generating ideas, but it has some advantages over group brainstorming where people shout out their ideas in a group. One advantage is that the blocking effects found in face-to-face brainstorming (e.g., evaluation apprehension and competition for speaking time) are reduced when people write their ideas privately rather than shouting them out.

Brainwriting is easier than group brainstorming because it does not require an experienced facilitator—nearly anyone can conduct a brainwriting session with confidence that the results will be useful.

Table 2.1 Method Scorecard for Brainwriting				
Overall Effort Required	Time for Planning and Conducting	Skill and Experience	Supplies and Equipment	Time for Data Analysis
▮▯▯▯▯	▮▯▯▯▯	▮▯▯▯▯	▮▯▯▯▯	▮▯▯▯▯
Most Useful During These Project Phases:				
✓ Problem Definition	✓ Requirements	✓ Conceptual Design	Detailed Design	Implementation

There are two general types of brainwriting: individual (sometimes called "nominal") and interactive. During individual brainwriting participants are given a question or topic and simply list their ideas privately for a specified period of time without discussion. You could consider free listing (see Chapter 1 on Brainstorming) where you ask a group to list as many ideas as possible to a question, as one type of individual brainwriting. All the ideas are collected, again without discussion, and clear duplicates are eliminated.

For interactive (group) brainwriting, participants are asked to do the following:

1. Write ideas on a page for a specified time (usually several minutes).
2. Pass their pages with ideas to the next person in the group on a signal from the brainwriting facilitator.
3. Silently read the ideas from the preceding person and add new ideas to the list without speaking to anyone else.
4. Pass the pages with ideas from the first two people to another person.
5. Repeat the process several more times and until the allotted time has run out.
6. Hand in the ideas to the brainwriting facilitator.

At the end of the interactive brainwriting session, all the ideas can be collected for future review or posted for review immediately. Participants can then "vote" on the best ideas or use another approach to determine what ideas to consider further.

This chapter will focus primarily on interactive brainwriting which involves a small group of participants, and unlike individual brainwriting, provides some synergy of ideas because each person reads the ideas of others before listing new ideas.

Brainwriting, Shoes, and a Swimming Pool

If you are short on time and want to get ideas for a large group, you can use individual or interactive brainwriting almost anywhere. While researching examples of brainwriting, this author ran across a story about a person who wanted to get ideas about a new customer relationship manager (CRM) tool at an international meeting, but had only a short time to do it and too many people (about 20) to do traditional group brainstorming. So he gave colleagues the question about CRMs and a template for listing ideas and sent them away for 15 minutes to generate ideas. People wrote up their ideas outside, then got together in an empty swimming pool to discuss and categorize the ideas. It was windy so they used their shoes to keep the various piles of related brainwriting ideas from flying away.

By the end of the session in the swimming pool, the group had dozens of related ideas grouped into about 40 piles.

Interactive brainwriting sessions are generally short, lasting from 10 to 20 minutes. However, the brainwriting method can be used online and last for days or weeks as colleagues generate new ideas that add to or enhance existing items (Dennis & Williams, 2003).

2.2 WHEN SHOULD YOU USE BRAINWRITING?

You can use brainwriting to:

- Generate ideas and solutions to problems with relatively large groups.
- Elicit ideas from groups that do not get along too well.
- Elicit questions from an internal or external group when you have limited time (say 5−15 minutes).
- Elicit input from quiet individuals.
- Elicit input in countries, corporate cultures, or environments where traditional group brainstorming may not be accepted (Geschka, 1996).

Brainwriting is most useful during the early stages of the product design cycle when you are generating ideas or solutions to design problems, but brainwriting can be used at any time during product design to generate ideas or solutions to problems. For example, if you encounter a serious problem late in development you could use brainwriting to get ideas from the product team or other stakeholders.

Using Brainwriting to Get Perspectives from Different Product Groups

Brainwriting can be used to gather questions that different groups, like developers, product managers, and user experience designers, have about users and their work.

A simple technique for understanding what different groups want to know about users is to ask colleagues at various team meetings to write down questions that they would like answered when you make your next site visit. You might, for example, use brainwriting at a managers' meeting where you ask the managers to write down three questions they have about users and then pass those questions on to the person sitting beside them. This second person lists three more questions, and so on, for three to four quick rounds. You could also just ask each person to write down three questions and hand them in after a few minutes using individual brainwriting if time is really limited, but the interactive approach might stimulate some additional questions as people read what others have written.

You could repeat this with software engineers, technical writers, quality engineers, sales agents, and technical support teams to see if different groups ask different questions or have different perspectives.

An analysis of the questions from the different groups could reveal themes, biases, or real gaps in understanding about users and their work and you can use the questions as input to site visits, questionnaires, interviews, and other methods.

2.2.1 Strengths
- Can be used to generate questions and ideas quickly during short meetings.
- Requires little training for participants or facilitators.
- Minimal facilitation is required unlike group brainstorming where a trained facilitator is recommended.

- Can produce more ideas than traditional group brainstorming (Paulus & Brown, 2003).
- Can be combined with group brainstorming and other creativity techniques to increase the number of ideas generated for a particular topic or problem (Spreng, 2007).
- Reduces the possibility for interpersonal conflict in contentious groups (VanGundy, 1984).
- Is a way to support reticent colleagues who would not necessarily speak up in group brainstorming.
- Reduces the possibility of social conformity (however, brainwriting doesn't eliminate conformity completely as some people may conform to known positions or solutions even when their ideas are not subject to direct group scrutiny).
- Reduces anxiety when you are working in a culture (or with a multi-cultural group) where brainstorming participants might be embarrassed to express novel or unusual ideas face-to-face.
- Reduces the likelihood of evaluation apprehension and production blocking.

2.2.2 Weaknesses
- It is less well known than the group brainstorming method.
- It is not as social as group brainstorming. Participants write their ideas without talking to anyone else.
- May not be as good as traditional group brainstorming for team-building (VanGundy, 1984).
- Participants may feel that they cannot fully express their ideas in writing.
- Handwriting can be somewhat difficult to decipher for the person who has to transcribe and interpret the output.

2.3 PROCEDURES AND PRACTICAL ADVICE ON INTERACTIVE BRAINWRITING

2.3.1 Planning an Interactive Brainwriting Session
1. **Develop a short (several-minute) introduction to brainwriting.** The word "brainwriting" will be new to almost everyone and you'll see a few curious faces when you first announce this method. Having an outline of key points about brainwriting is quite useful. The basic points to include in an introduction for brainwriting are as follows:
   - Brainwriting is a variation on brainstorming.

- It is a parallel process that enables a small (or large) group to generate many ideas in a short period of time.
- All ideas should be legible.
- No names are attached to the ideas.
- The only materials required are pen and paper or pages with sticky notes.
- Participants get to see other ideas which can trigger new ideas or modifications of existing ideas.

2. **Develop the question or topic that you are going to pose to the participants.** If you have time, you could print out pages with the question or topic at the top of otherwise blank pages so your participants keep their focus during the session.

3. **Practice the process with a small group of friendly colleagues before you use this method with an unknown audience.** Refine your instructions. Ask your practice group to comment on the brainwriting process.

4. **Decide how the lists of items created by participants will be distributed (placed in a pile and redistributed or handed to the next participant or some other method of distribution) and how long each writing period will last.** These might seem like minor logistical issues, but they are important because you want the process to be perceived as smooth, efficient, and professional. The particular method that you use will depend somewhat on the type of group you are working with.

5. **Remember that the most important thing about brainwriting or traditional brainstorming is what you will do with the results.** Plan how you will record, track, and get input on the brainwriting items. You might publish a list of the ideas or post them on a wall where people can make comments or add to the brainwriting list.

2.3.2 Conducting an Interactive Brainwriting Session

1. **(Optional). Send participants an email with the brainwriting question or topic and ask the participants to list two to three ideas.** This minimal homework is meant to get the participants thinking about the topic. This is feasible with small groups but not so feasible if you are doing this at a large meeting.

2. **Describe the topic of interest and how long the session will last.** For example, your brainwriting session could be used to generate ideas for a new product or questions about users and their work. Write the brainwriting topic on a board or on flip chart so that everyone

can see it during the session and make sure that everyone understands what you are asking.

3. **Hand out sheets of paper or forms for the group to use for brainwriting**. Table 2.1 shows an example that is adapted from one at www.creatingMinds.org (n.d.). If you use a brainwriting form, fill a page with rectangles that are large enough to contain an idea. Tell the participants to fill in several blanks with their ideas and then pass the form on to someone else or just have each person fill out as many blanks as possible until time is called for that iteration. In Table 2.1, the participant came up with 11 ideas related to the question posed by the owner, Chauncey Wilson.

4. **Describe the brainwriting process to the group**. The general points that you should cover are as follows:
   a. Each person will spend a fixed amount of time (a few minutes) writing ideas on the pages. Then the pages will be:
      1. (Option 1) Shuffled and redistributed.
      2. (Option 2) Passed to the person next to you.
   b. The ideas should be generated quickly without concern for how "good" they are. Stress that quantity is more important than quality—just as in traditional brainstorming. Also, the facilitator should ask that the ideas be written (or printed) legibly.
   c. The pages and ideas do not have to be identified with the names of participants.
   d. When the brainwriting session starts, each person begins writing until asked the facilitator gives a time signal. When time is called, everyone hands their page to someone else or puts it in a pile and then draws another one out.
   e. The second person should read all the ideas on the page from the first person and add new ideas. The facilitator should stress that it is important to read all the previous ideas on a sheet to help stimulate the production of new ideas.
   f. The process is continued for about three to five iterations that last from 2 to 5 minutes per iteration.

●●●───

Tip: Make the First Round of Interactive Brainwriting Longer than the Remaining Rounds

The first round should be longer than the remaining rounds because there is some cognitive inertia to overcome when you confront a blank page.

Table 2.3 Template for the Brainwriting 6-3-5 Variation			
Brainwriting Topic or Question: (For example, How do I ...?)			
Participant	Idea 1	Idea 2	Idea 3
1			
2			
3			
4			
5			
6			

specific topic or problem, and then pass the form on to the next person in the group after 5 minutes. This process is repeated six times over 30 minutes. The end result yields, ideally, 90 ideas per session—6(people) × 3 (ideas) × 5(iterations).

2.4.3 The Card-Exchange Technique

Geschka (1983, 1996) proposed a brainwriting technique called the card-exchange technique. In this variation of brainwriting, ideas are written on cards using dark markers and placed on one side of the participants. When participants want some stimulation for new ideas, they pick up one or more cards from the adjacent participants, read through them, then add new ideas on new cards (one idea per card). This process lasts for about 20 minutes. At the end of the session, the cards are pinned or stuck on a wall and adhesive dots are attached to the most promising ideas. The idea here is that there is no time pressure on how long you work on the cards. You write a card and place it in a pile, then write another, and when you want to get a few new ideas, you read the cards from your neighbor.

The use of cards rather than sheets makes it easy to vote on the ideas or create an affinity diagram. Geschka (1996) reported that the brainwriting approach is preferred by Germans because it allows participants to develop one's own ideas better and does not have the problems with group dynamics that can occur in group brainstorming.

2.4.4 One Idea, Quick Pass

In this variation of brainwriting (which could be based on a "speed dating" metaphor), each person writes one idea and passes it on to the next person who adds another idea. If anyone on the brainwriting team is slow in writing an idea, the next person can start a new sheet and pass it on to the next person. At the end of the quick pass brainwriting time, all sheets are collected, put on display, and the items are evaluated for further consideration.

2.4.5 Crawford Slip Method

Dettmer (2003) and Higgins (1994) described a form of brainwriting called the Crawford Slip Method (CSM) (it is also called Crawford Slip Writing) which can be used with small or very large groups (dozens to hundreds of people). This method was invented in the 1920s by Dr. C. C. Crawford of the University of Southern California who had exacting (some say obsessive) rules about how to apply his slip method. An advantage of this method is that you can use it to capture a great deal of data from large groups like those you might find at a user or professional conference. The basic CSM procedure is:

1. Hand out a stack of at least 25 small slips of paper to all the participants.
2. Present the group with a problem area, the overall problem, and some additional statements or problem questions that elaborate on the overall problem.

   Box 2.1 is an example of a "problem area" that would be presented to participants. For example, in Box 2.1, the problem question asks participants to list difficulties and failures encountered while trying to establish a usability engineering process.
3. Ask people to write their ideas related to the problem area on the slips of paper—one idea to each slip so the slips can be sorted easily. Each idea should be a single sentence. For the problem question in Box 2.1, you might have ideas on the slips like:
   • Upper management has not officially endorsed usability as a required part of the development process.
   • There is no usability sign-off.
   • There is no category of "usability bug" in the bug database.
   • We weren't invited to the managers' weekly meeting.
   • People in our company don't realize that you can evaluate concepts using paper prototypes early in design.
4. Give people 5–10 min to write their ideas on the slips (or wait until you notice that the writing has slowed down) and then collect the slips.

Box 2.1 Problem Statement Example for a CSM Session

Crawford Slip Method Example
Problem Area: Integrating usability into the development process
Overall Problem: Usability is often done too late at our company and customers are clamoring for more usability
Problem Question: What difficulties or failures have you and your colleague had in implementing usability engineering into the development process?
Replies to the Problem Question: Write each difficulty or failure related to the problem area on a separate slip.

5. Have a designated team sort the ideas based on specific criteria like feasibility, resources required, importance, frequency, and amount of training required. If the group is very large, this can be done off-line rather than in the particular meeting. Consider drawing a random sample if you have notes from a large group and report preliminary ideas based on the random sample (Mycoted, n.d.).

There are some specific rules in the CSM for writing replies to the question that is posed. The most important rules are (Higgins, 1994):

- **Write only one sentence per card.** You might amend this to be "one idea per card." Crawford was a stickler on this point because multiple sentences might mean different things and multiple sentences on the same card complicated sorting and analysis.
- **Avoid ambiguous pronouns like "it" and "this."** Be specific so the ideas will be understood days or weeks later. This is a good rule for any type of ideation output.
- **Spell out acronyms and avoid abbreviations.** The rationale here is similar to the previous bullet point. Some of the people writing the slips may assume that everyone knows what an abbreviation like "sm" means, but the reality is that some people won't know what it means (would you have guessed that "sm" meant "square meter"?).
- **Ask the people generating the slips to write for people who may not be experts in the particular domain of interest.** For example, you could ask a group of architects to describe problems they encounter with their architectural design software in terms that non-architects would understand.

The CSM is useful when group conflict might reduce the number of ideas generated by participants. The cards that participants fill out are not distributed to anyone (unlike the interactive brainwriting approach) although the final results are generally published for the group. Another advantage of this method is that quiet people are not intimidated by more vocal colleagues. For more information on the CSM see Dettmer (2003).

2.5 MAJOR ISSUES IN THE USE OF BRAINWRITING

2.5.1 Why Use Brainwriting When Our Team Already Knows About Group Brainstorming?

Paulus and Brown (2003) conducted research showing that brainwriting generates about 40% more ideas than traditional group brainstorming. Their research suggests that this difference is probably due to the many distractions possible in group brainstorming that can reduce the total quantity of ideas (see Chapter 1 on brainstorming for more details). There are also issues of subconscious conformity, fear about pleasing one's manager, inhibitions about speaking out in public, and the tendency of groups to view themselves as more effective than individuals even though groups often generate fewer ideas than individuals who are brainstorming alone (thus groups may overestimate their effectiveness and stop sooner than individuals).

2.6 DATA ANALYSIS

2.6.1 Types of Data

The types of data that can be collected during brainwriting include:

- A list of ideas, questions, or other statements related to the brainwriting topic.
- (Optional) Elaborations and explanations of ideas during the review process.
- (Optional) Grouping and prioritization of ideas into categories at the end of brainwriting sessions.
- Feedback on the brainwriting method.

2.6.2 Analysis Techniques

2.6.2.1 Listing Ideas

All the ideas from a brainstorming session can be listed in a spreadsheet, word processor, or specialized tools like PathMaker® or

Inspiration. If you have numbered the items sequentially as they were generated, your list would be chronological. To facilitate recall, days, weeks, or even months later when you look through this list, you can annotate the list with clarifications and brief explanations of any unusual terms or abbreviations.

2.6.2.2 Grouping Ideas from Brainwriting
Affinity diagramming can be used to organize ideas into related groups. See Chapter 1 for some details on affinity diagramming.

2.6.2.3 Rating or Ranking Brainwriting Ideas
The process of brainwriting focuses on generating ideas. For some purposes, you may want to prioritize ideas against specific criteria. One simple approach you can use for prioritizing data is to apply a simple criterion (or a few criteria) to each idea and eliminate the ideas that don't meet the criterion. A criterion would include the word "should", for example, "the idea should be compatible with the existing user interface," "the idea should not extend the schedule," "the idea should be easily learned," and "the idea should minimize errors." You might do something like rate each idea on a 0-to-5 scale where 0 means "does not meet the criterion at all" and 5 is "meets the criterion quite well." Once the brainwriting team has chosen items to be investigated further, individuals or team could be assigned to examine the costs and benefits of chosen items or assigned to evaluate them on specific dimensions (costs, benefits to the users, time to implement, and so on).

The nominal group rating technique described in Chapter 1 on brainstorming is sometimes used after a brainwriting session as a method for prioritizing the ideas that emerged. The facilitator would ask each member of the brainwriting team to rate privately all the ideas as a 1 (low), 2 (medium), or 3 (high). The ideas with the highest average rating would get the highest priority.

2.6.2.4 Decision Matrix
A decision matrix (sometimes called a "prioritization matrix") uses the ideas from brainwriting and a set of criteria for rating the ideas. Some software products include a "decision matrix" where the ideas are listed on one axis and the criteria on another axis (Table 2.4). Participants would rate each item according to how well the item meets the criteria. This assumes that you are reasonably sure of the

Idea/ Criteria	Criterion 1	Criterion 2	Criterion 3	Criterion ...	Criterion N	Sum	Mean Rating
Idea 1							
Idea 2							
Idea 3							
Idea 4							
Idea ...	...	...	...	...	...	...	...
Idea n							

Table 2.4 Layout of a Prioritization Matrix

criteria for deciding which ideas to carry forward. Criteria that you might use in this table include:

- Cost
- Skill required to implement the idea (you might have a great idea, but now the personnel to implement the idea)
- Technical feasibility
- Consistency with existing products
- Time to code

2.7 WHAT DO YOU NEED TO USE THE BRAINWRITING METHOD?

2.7.1 Personnel, Participants, and Training

You need a small, diverse group of people for an interactive brainwriting session where ideas will be passed to others. A facilitator or "brainwriting lead" is useful for explaining the process and keeping the brainwriting session efficient, but you don't need a professional facilitator.

Training requirements for the brainwriting facilitator are low because brainwriting requires fewer social and technical skills than group brainstorming. Participants do not talk as they generate ideas so there is almost no group discussion to facilitate during the brainwriting session. The procedures described in this chapter should provide you with enough background to try this method or one of the variations with a high probability of success.

Training requirements for participants are low. A short introduction to the brainwriting method and a clear statement of the rules for the process are about all that is needed.

2.7.2 Hardware and Software

Brainwriting can be done as a paper-and-pencil exercise or you could use a variety of electronic brainstorming (EBS) tools like listservs, chat systems, wikis, or other collaboration tools where participants can type in their ideas for viewing by everyone. As development groups get large, EBS is more advantageous because it reduces the cognitive overhead associated with turn-taking and thinking while others are talking during group brainstorming. The value of EBS increases with group size and geographical diversity.

One lost-cost approach for remote brainwriting is to use a collaborative spreadsheet like Google Spreadsheet where individuals can be assigned a column and then enter their items in that column while also seeing what others have typed in as inspiration. A collaborative spreadsheet is something that could be kept open for a period of time so people can see other ideas and add theirs when convenient. Figure 2.1 shows an example of a spreadsheet with questions that different colleagues want to ask users. They can log in to the spreadsheet, read what others have listed in their columns, and add new items.

2.7.3 Documents and Materials

The only materials you need for face-to-face interactive brainwriting are sheets of paper, pens or markers, easels with poster paper, and some way to attach the pages of brainwriting to a wall or other surface that can serve as a temporary idea display. One variant suggested by

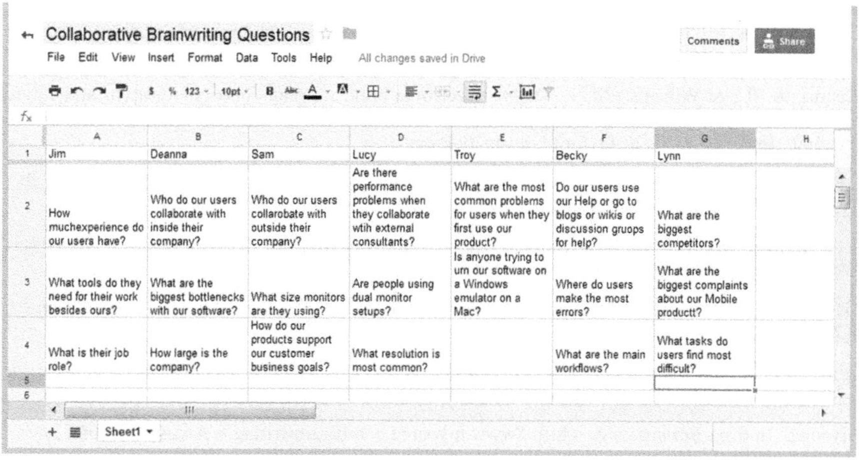

Figure 2.1 Remote collaborative brainwriting using a distributed spreadsheet.

Bayle (2004) might be to put ideas on Post-It® Notes and then put the ideas on a piece of paper so they can be passed around. When the session is over, the ideas can easily be transferred to a public viewing area and voted on, prioritized, or grouped. Simple tabular forms like the brainwriting sheet shown in Box 2.1 can be used for group brainwriting.

RECOMMENDED READINGS

Geschka, H. (1996). Creativity techniques in Germany. *Creativity and Innovation Management,* 5(2), 87−92. Geschka explains why brainwriting is a more culturally acceptable method in Germany for ideation than group brainstorming and also describes two variations of brainwriting as well as other creativity techniques. Geschka lists other techniques for ideation and problem solving.

Paulus, P. B. & Brown, V. R. (2003). Enhancing ideational creativity in groups: Lessons from research on brainstorming. In P. B. Paulus & B. A. Nijstad (Eds.), *Group creativity: Innovation through collaboration* (pp. 110−136). Oxford, UK: Oxford University Press. Paulus and Nijstad have edited a book that captures a wide range of research into group creativity. Much of the book deals with brainstorming, brainwriting, and related methods for generating ideas and solutions to problems. While the book is loaded with research and some theory, most chapters have a set of practical implications for group creativity methods like brainstorming and brainwriting. The book discusses both face-to-face and electronic methods and their respective strengths and weaknesses. The book highlights how social inhibitors can affect creative productivity and provides some research-based tips on how to overcome these inhibitors.

REFERENCES

Bayle, E. (2004, April). Using post-it notes for brainwriting (Personal communication).

Brahm, C., & Kleiner, B. H. (1996). Advantages and disadvantages of group decision-making. *Team Performance Management, 2*(1), 30−35.

CreatingMinds.org. (n.d.). *Brainwriting.* <http://creatingminds.org/tools/brainwriting.htm> Accessed 12.10.12.

Dennis, A. R., & Williams, M. L. (2003). Electronic brainstorming: Theory, research, and future directions. In P. B. Paulus, & B. A. Nijstad (Eds.), *Group creativity: Innovation through collaboration* (pp. 160−180). Oxford, UK: Oxford University Press.

Dettmer, H. W. (2003). *Brainpower networking using the Crawford slip method.* Victoria, BC: Trafford Publishing.

Geschka, H. (1983). Creativity techniques in product planning and development: A view from West Germany. *R&D Management, 13*(3), 169−183.

Geschka, H. (1996). Creativity techniques in Germany. *Creativity and Innovation Management,* 5(2), 87−92.

Higgins, J. M. (1994). *101 Creative problem solving techniques: The handbook of new ideas for business.* Winter Park, FL: The New Management Publishing Company.

Mycoted. (n.d.)a. *Brainwriting.* <http://www.mycoted.com/Brainwriting> Accessed 01.06.12.

Mycoted. (n.d.)b. *Crawford slip writing.* <http://www.mycoted.com/Crawford_Slip_Writing> Accessed 28.01.10.

Osborn, A. F. (1963). *Applied imagination: Principles and procedures of creative problem-solving* (3rd revised ed.). New York, NY: Charles Scribner's Sons.

Paulus, P. B., & Brown, V. R. (2003). Enhancing ideational creativity in groups: Lessons from research on brainstorming. In P. B. Paulus, & B. A. Nijstad (Eds.), *Group creativity: Innovation through collaboration* (pp. 110–136). Oxford, UK: Oxford University Press.

Spreng, K. P. (2007). Enhancing creativity in brainstorming for successful problem solving. HOT Topics. <http://hot.carleton.ca/hot-topics/articles/brainstorming/> Accessed 01.06.08.

VanGundy, A. B. (1984). *Managing group creativity: A modular approach to problem solving.* New York, NY: AMACOM, Division of the American Management Association.

CHAPTER *3*

Braindrawing

Alternate Names: Braindrawing, brain sketching, gallery method, visual brainstorming.

Related Methods: Affinity diagramming, brainstorming, brainwriting, metaphor brainstorming, storyboards.

3.1 OVERVIEW OF BRAINDRAWING

Braindrawing (Usability Body of Knowledge, n.d.) is a method of graphic brainstorming and problem solving where participants create and modify rough sketches quickly to generate ideas or solve visual layout problems. For example, braindrawing could be used to come up with ideas for icons that will represent abstract functions in toolbars, menus, or ribbons. Braindrawing can also be used to explore layouts for dialog boxes, Web pages, and mobile screens.

Table 3.1 is a scorecard that highlights the relative investment needed to conduct a braindrawing session and when braindrawing is most useful.

The basic procedure for braindrawing involves the following steps:

1. **State a visual design question or topic for a small group of participants and explain that you would like them to generate ideas by creating rough sketches.** Here are three examples of visual design questions and topics that would be appropriate for braindrawing:
   a. What kind of image can we use in a graphical toolbar to represent the feature "render this drawing"?
   b. We are planning on redoing the home page for our set of products. What ideas do you have for a new home page design that will appeal to our three primary personas?
   c. What kind of user interface would allow users to compare multiple products on different features and attributes?

Table 3.1 Method Scorecard for Braindrawing

Overall Effort Required	Time for Planning and Conducting	Skill and Experience	Supplies and Equipment	Time for Data Analysis
▉☐☐☐☐	▉☐☐☐☐	▉☐☐☐☐	▉☐☐☐☐	▉☐☐☐☐

Most Useful During These Project Phases:				
✓ Problem Definition	✓ Requirements	✓ Conceptual Design	Detailed Design	Implementation

2. **At a signal from the facilitator, a sketch (or page of sketches) is passed to another person who then enhances or adds something to the sketch or creates a new sketch.** After a designated time, each person passes the accumulated sketches on to yet another person.

3. **Repeat the sketch-then-pass process three to six times.** For example, you might do five iterations of braindrawing with the first iteration lasting 10 minutes (the first person has a blank page and might need more time to get started) followed by 4-, 5-minutes enhancement iterations.

4. **At the end of a braindrawing session, all the sketches created by the group are posted in an "art gallery" where colleagues and participants in the braindrawing session can review the sketches and discuss which ideas should be considered further.** Gause and Weinberg (1989, p. 123) suggested that "each drawing [be] presented by someone who didn't contribute to it." You could also have a facilitator engage the team in a discussion about the ideas embodied in each sketch.

5. **(Optional) The group votes on the best ideas and then prioritizes them further at the end of the session or at a separate session.** The ideas can also be evaluated by a different group.

You can use braindrawing to generate ideas for icons or graphics that you need for your product. For example, you might ask members of the product team (or students or graphic designers) to generate ideas for a concept or feature like "filtering bad data from the database." In this type of braindrawing, the participants each draw a rough concept sketch, then the next person looks at the first sketch and tries to improve it or draws a new idea. Figure 3.1 is an example of a single braindrawing page that includes sketches for a "filter" icon from three people.

You can use braindrawing with members of the product team or as a participatory design method with users or domain specialists (Muller, Haslwanter, & Dayton, 1997).

Braindrawing sessions are generally short, lasting from 10 to 60 minutes depending on the complexity of the visual problem. This would include time to explain the process, time for several rounds of drawing, and an initial review to extract ideas from the braindrawings.

Figure 3.1 Example page from a braindrawing session to get ideas how to represent the concept "filter."

3.2 WHEN SHOULD YOU USE BRAINDRAWING?

Braindrawing is useful for:

- Generating visual design concepts.
- Eliciting requirements or ideas that may have been missed in traditional brainstorming.
- Generating ideas from groups who prefer non-verbal approaches to problem solving.

- Working on visual concepts with children (Keller-Mathers & Puccio, 2000). Drawing is a natural activity for most children, so braindrawing could be used as a form of low-tech prototyping or ideation.
- Communicating what different members of the product team believe are important features or visual issues for a new product or service.

The braindrawing method is most useful during the early stages of concept development and requirements gathering to generate a range of design options. This method complements text-oriented idea generation methods like group brainstorming and interactive brainwriting. The method could also be applied during the early stages of user interface design to get ideas about layout or solve a visual design problem.

3.2.1 Strengths
- It is simple and requires minimal training, materials, and preparation.
- May be more powerful than words for generating ideas for graphics Creatingminds.org (n.d.).
- May communicate complex ideas better than words and reduce comments like "that isn't what I meant" which can occur in standard brainstorming sessions. Gause and Weinberg (1989) suggested that the use of visual braindrawing can reduce the miscommunication and verbal violence that sometimes results from ambiguous descriptions of ideas that follow from standard group brainstorming.
- Can be used with both children and adults.

Children Can Use It Too

Keller-Matthews and Puccio (2000) applied braindrawing to help primary school children express their creativity. In their approach which they call "the amazing braindrawing machine," children are asked to create "many, varied, and unusual machines using braindrawing" (p. 17).

Teachers start the exercise by posting pictures of many kinds of machines on a wall. Teachers also bring some machines to the classroom and let the students touch the machines to engage their tactile sense. Then they give students a braindrawing form and ask them to draw three ideas for "supermachines" like a phone with a TV and oven, cars with built-in bridges for crossing streams or alarm clocks with toasters that also cook eggs. The students are told to be as creative as possible.

After students create three ideas, they hand their forms to other students and encourage them to draw three more "supermachines." They are encouraged to use and combine ideas from other children. The children are encouraged to think about ideas rather than "my idea." This exercise is really one of creating novel user interfaces and is very similar to the "adult" version described in this chapter.

3.2.2 Weaknesses
- May be viewed as frivolous (similar complaints are often voiced about paper prototyping).
- There are no definitive techniques for analyzing and interpreting the ideas from a braindrawing session in the literature (some are suggested at the end of this chapter).
- Some participants may get fixated on one idea and draw the same thing repeatedly with trivial variations.
- May be uncomfortable for participants who are shy about their "artwork." The passing of drawings to another person might be somewhat threatening if you are passing things to your manager or to the group's visual designer.
- Untrained facilitators may not be adept at limiting comments on the sketches during the iterations or keeping extraneous comments from affecting the participants.

3.3 PROCEDURES AND PRACTICAL ADVICE ON THE BRAINDRAWING METHOD
3.3.1 Planning a Braindrawing Session
1. **Develop a short (several minute) introduction to braindrawing.** This introduction describes the basic procedure for braindrawing.
2. **Choose a location where you have space to display the results of the brainstorming.**
3. **Bring a stack of paper and markers to the meeting.** If you are using easels for drawing, bring some of the poster-sized paper with an adhesive edge to make it easy to display the drawings later. Consider bringing a timer to the session so you can time each round of braindrawing.

Tip

Provide the participants with an example of some braindrawings that will ease their anxiety about sketching in public. Showing participants examples of rough sketches from non-artists has a calming influence on people who might consider themselves (as this author does) artistically impaired.

3.3.2 Conducting a Braindrawing Session

1. **Describe the goal or problem statement for the session, for example, "generate visual ideas for an advanced search engine interface" or "sketch what the new home page might look like."** You might also address specific problems like "how should we arrange the menu items?" or "what icon should we use to represent the new 'filter' function?" and have each person sketch out ideas for the new interface, menu arrangement, or icon.

2. **Explain the ground rules for the braindrawing session.** The rules are similar to those used for brainstorming and brainwriting with slight changes to reflect the graphical nature of the task:
   a. Generate as many ideas as possible and do not worry about your sketching prowess; block diagrams, rough ideas, and crooked lines are OK.
   b. No criticism of anyone's ideas or drawing skills.
   c. You can create new sketches at any time or enhance something that another person has drawn.
   d. You can use a few words to describe a concept, but the diagrams should not have too much text.

3. **Assure the participants that the quality of their sketches is not an issue.** The purposes of braindrawing are to generate ideas, think outside the box, and discover requirements that may have been missed using less visual means of idea generation.

4. **Tell people how much time they will have for each round of drawing.** The first round of sketching should be a little longer than succeeding rounds (e.g., 10 vs 5 minutes). The amount of time you let people sketch during a round will depend on the complexity of your problem. Sketching rounds could last 5 or 30 minutes. Let the participants know when there are a few minutes left so they can complete their sketches.

5. **Start the braindrawing session and record the time.** Give a clear signal to start the brainstorming. When a round has ended ask participants to pass their drawing to the person on their left or right. You can also put the sketches in a pile and redistribute them to the

group at the end of each round (without giving anyone their last drawing) to minimize anxiety about your manager or someone else seeing your raw sketches. Repeat this procedure several times (four to five iterations are reasonable).

6. **When the braindrawing is complete, put all the sketches in a public gallery and discuss the ideas that emerged.** The facilitator could lead the discussion, or you could have different participants walk through the sketches and describe some of the ideas that emerge. This review session should be explanatory and descriptive and not critical. The purpose here is to extract good ideas. A critical review or some additional braindrawing iterations that build on the good ideas can follow this step.

7. **Review the sketches in terms of what is most important—new requirements, better ways to do something, new additions to the interface that build on what is already there, and so on.** This way, the sketches are reviewed in a meaningful manner.

8. **Have a good notetaker take notes on comments, additional ideas, and questions that are posed by the group about the braindrawings.** It is often useful to use a digital camera to take a picture of each sketch and then insert the picture into the notes.

9. **Conduct a critical evaluation of ideas that emerged as a group and create a deliverable that encapsulates the evaluation.** A critical evaluation might consist of consensus judgments on ideas that have promise or you might have the participants put colored dots on the sketches with promising ideas and collect those sketches for further consideration.

3.3.3 After the Braindrawing Session

1. **Capture all the ideas and record which ideas received votes for future attention.** Catalog all the ideas, preferably in some kind of database, because some that were not considered important at first, may become important later. If you are working at a remote site, consider bringing a small scanner with you and scanning the drawings so you can post them in your product team's intranet.

2. **Develop a plan for investigating the important items in more detail.** You might, for example, have a group create a matrix of potential solutions and look at the costs and benefits of each and then narrow the list of ideas to the ones that seem feasible under your current constraints.

3.4 VARIATIONS AND EXTENSIONS TO BRAINDRAWING

3.4.1 Move the Sketchers Rather than Move the Sketches

If you have a small group, you might consider using easels with poster paper and have the participants move from easel to easel to do their sketching rather than having them hand their sketches over to the next person in the braindrawing group (Muller, Haslwanter, & Dayton, 1997).

3.4.2 The Gallery Method

Another variation on braindrawing is the "gallery method" (MycoTed. com, n.d.) where people work on a large sheet of paper and then walk around at a break to get ideas from the sketches of others. This is similar to the first variation where participants move from easel to easel—the difference here is that they use the sketches of others for inspiration (there is no ownership of ideas) and then come back and work more on their own sketch rather than modifying the sketches of others.

1. Write a goal or problem statement on large sheets of paper or flip charts. Have one large sheet for each person in the group. Plan for five to eight participants.
2. Review the goal or problem statement to ensure that everyone understands the purpose of the braindrawing session. Discuss any questions that emerge.
3. Have each person work in front of one of the large sheets of paper sketching or writing possible solutions to the problem. Ask each person to draw and write large and legibly.

Weblink

To see another variation on braindrawing that uses "doodling" as a braindrawing approach see http://creatingminds.org/tools/braindrawing.htm

---

4. After a period of time, say 20 minutes, ask people to take a short break, walk around, look at the sketches of others and then go back and continue work on their sketches using ideas from the sketches of the other participants.
5. When people run short of ideas, take another break and then resume working on the sketches again.
6. Review the sketches and extract useful ideas.

3.5 MAJOR ISSUES IN THE USE OF BRAINDRAWING

3.5.1 Artistic Anxiety

Braindrawing is an activity that can be playful and engaging for members of a product team or groups of users. However, there can be some discomfort the first time this method is used. This discomfort arises from fears that one's "art" or ideas are not very good. Facilitators need to reassure people that their artistic skills will not be criticized or evaluated. Some examples of rough sketches can reduce this artistic anxiety. If you have a graphic designer on your team, you might consider asking him or her to just observe so others don't feel intimidated by the presence of a professional.

The presence of managers might inhibit some braindrawing participants. If you have managers in the mix of participants, you might brief them to be sensitive to the artistic skills (or lack of skills) of others.

3.5.2 Using Braindrawing with Children

Braindrawing is sometimes mentioned as a useful method for creative problem solving with children. The key to using braindrawing with children is to eliminate fears of individual evaluation ("no one is going to grade your pictures") (Keller-Mathers & Puccio, 2000). Actually, the statement of not "grading" pictures applies to all ages of participants.

3.6 DATA ANALYSIS

3.6.1 Types of Data

The types of data that can be collected during braindrawing sessions include:

- The sketches themselves.
- The comments that occur during the review of the sketches.
- Common visual themes that emerge from the sketches
- A list of ideas and new requirements that emerge from the group review.

3.6.2 Analysis Techniques

3.6.2.1 Idea Extraction

During the walkthrough of the sketches, the notetaker can record comments on the sketches and circle ideas that seem promising. These walkthroughs can reveal assumptions about the visual problem and sometimes suggest visual components that might be useful for the final design. If your braindrawing session focused on a macro problem like ideas for a new home page, you will find that your sketches reveal requirements as well as visual layout ideas. For example, if you had your team sketch ideas for a page where you could order pizza for delivery, your participants drawings might suggest requirements like:

- Choice of delivery or pickup.
- A way to choose the time of the order.
- A display of restrictions for delivery and pizza creation.
- Multiple toppings on a single pizza (e.g., ½ meat; ½ mushroom).
- Coupon redemption.
- Allergy warnings.
- Nutritional information.

3.6.2.2 Voting, Rating, or Ranking

Participants or other colleagues can vote on, rate, or rank the visual ideas that best support the goal of the braindrawing session. A simple technique for choosing good ideas is to have your participants (or others) take some adhesive dots and stick the dots on the sketches that have useful ideas. The sketches with the most dots would be candidates for refinement and use in the product. A more formal approach to data analysis would be to scan in the sketches and ask colleagues to rate or rank the sketches based on important criteria.

3.7 WHAT DO YOU NEED TO USE BRAINDRAWING?

3.7.1 Personnel, Participants, and Training

You need a small team of five to ten people who will be involved in the project. Having a diverse team is helpful for getting a range of ideas. You need a facilitator who will run the session and a notetaker to capture the ideas and discussions of the braindrawings. The facilitator should be encouraging and facile at moderating a semi-structured discussion of the sketches at the end of the braindrawing session.

Training requirements for the facilitator are low to moderate. The facilitator must be good at introducing this new visual approach for generating design ideas and persuading management that it is useful and effective.

Training requirements for participants are low. This method generally requires only a short introduction and a few examples as "training."

3.7.2 Hardware and Software

Braindrawing requires no special hardware or software. Remote conferencing tools like GoToMeeting, WebEx, Centra, and LiveMeeting that allow people to sketch on a virtual whiteboard could be used for remote braindrawing exercises.

You might consider scanning in braindrawing diagrams, putting them into a database, and tagging them with appropriate keywords and other metadata for future use as ideas that aren't useful now might be useful at a later date.

3.7.3 Documents and Materials

The only materials you need are sheets of paper, pens or markers, easels with poster paper, and tape to attach the braindrawings to a wall or other surface that can serve as a temporary art gallery.

If you have people sketch on easels you will need one easel for each participant or small group of participants. Two people working together is reasonable, but when you go to three or more people trying to come up with a group sketch, the process can become inefficient because of the need to resolve differences and share the drawing implements rather than just drawing.

RECOMMENDED READINGS

Paulus, P. B., & Brown, V. R. (2003). Enhancing ideational creativity in groups: Lessons from research on brainstorming. In P. B. Paulus & B. A. Nijstad (Eds.), *Group creativity: Innovation through collaboration* (pp. 110–136). Oxford, UK: Oxford University Press. This edited book contains good general information on brainstorming techniques and also references on braindrawing and brainwriting. This book describes research and includes tips for practitioners at the end of most chapters.

Usability Body of Knowledge (BoK). (n.d.). *Braindrawing*. http://www.usabilitybok.org/braindrawing Accessed 28.10.12. There is an excellent summary of braindrawing in the Usability Body of Knowledge database.

REFERENCES

Creatingminds.org. (n.d.). *Braindrawing*. <http://creatingminds.org/tools/braindrawing.htm> Accessed 31.08.12.

Gause, D. C., & Weinberg, G. M. (1989). *Exploring requirements: Quality before design*. New York, NY: Dorset House.

Keller-Mathers, S., & Puccio, K. (2000). *Big tools for young thinkers: Using creative problem solving tools with primary students*. Waco, TX: Prufrock Press.

MycoTed.com. (n.d.). *Gallery method*. <http://www.mycoted.com/creativity/techniques/gallery.php> Accessed 28.10.12.

Muller, M. J., Haslwanter, J. H., & Dayton, T. (1997). Participatory practices in the software lifecycle. In M. Helander, T. K. Landauer, & P. V. Prabhu. (Eds.), *Handbook of human-computer interaction* (pp. 255–298). Amsterdam: Elsevier.

Paulus, P. B., & Brown, V. R. (2003). Enhancing ideational creativity in groups: Lessons from research on brainstorming. In P. B. Paulus, & B. A. Nijstad (Eds.), *Group creativity: Innovation through collaboration* (pp. 110–136). Oxford, UK: Oxford University Press.

Usability Body of Knowledge (BoK). (n.d.). *Braindrawing*. <http://www.usabilitybok.org/braindrawing> Accessed 28.10.12.

Printed and bound by CPI Group (UK) Ltd, Croydon, CR0 4YY

03/10/2024

01040413-0009